P9-DET-571

HOPKINSVILLE - CHRIS. CO.
PUBLIC LIBRARY
1101 BETHEL STREET
HOPKINSVILLE, KY. 42240

FE95

No Tears for Mao

NO TEARS FOR MAO:

GROWING UP IN THE CULTURAL REVOLUTION

NIU-NIU

Translated by Enne and Peter Amman

Academy Chicago Publishers

Published in 1995 by
Academy Chicago Publishers
363 W. Erie Street
Chicago, IL 60610

© Editions Robert Laffont, S.A., Paris, 1989

Printed and bound in the U.S.A.

No part of this book may be reproduced in any form
without the express written permission of the publisher.

Library of Congress Cataloging-in-Publication Data

Niu-Niu.
    [Pas de larmes pour Mao. English]
    No tears for Mao: growing up in the Cultural Revolution/Niu-Niu:
    translated by Peter and Enne Amman.
        p.   cm.
    ISBN 0-89733-410-8: $22.95
    1. Niu-Niu. 2. China—History—Cultural Revolution, 1966-1969—
    Personal narratives. I. Title.
    DS 778.7.N58 1994
    951.05'6—dc20   94-40601
                                                          CIP

# CONTENTS

Chapter 1
MY FIRST MEMORY

That was the year, the month, the very day. I was in the court-yard of our house in Chengdu, playing with my big sister, Mimi. Inside, my parents and grandparents were quietly chatting over tea. I remember the lovely flowers in the garden, the light wind that caressed my cheeks — suddenly the door flew open and a screaming hurricane roared past me.

It consisted of about fifteen or twenty men carrying rifles and waving their Little Red Books. I couldn't understand why they broke our windows and turned everything upside down in our house. I cried out, horribly afraid. When I ran towards my parents, the men formed a wall around them, beating them, screaming insults at them. I didn't understand the ugly words, all I saw was that these men were pointing their fingers at my father and mother.

"Papa! Mama!"

My stunned grandparents suddenly roused themselves as they heard our cries. They scooped Mimi and me into their arms, while one of the men bellowed, "Shut up, you little bitches!"

I saw my parents stammer something under the blows. My grandmother, suddenly panicked, put me down hastily and tried desperately to stop these savages. My grandfather begged them to stop, but they knocked him to the floor. At that point no one was paying any attention to Mimi and me.

Terribly frightened, I screamed. On all fours I crawled toward my parents; one of the men picked me up by the neck like a kitten and threw me aside.

After they had broken everything in the house, gathered everything that could be burned — our old paintings, books, papers, photographs — they stole the clothes, the furs, the jewelry and the two little golden Buddhas on the altar of our ancestors. They even wrecked our ancestral altar.

They jerked my parents' hands high behind their backs, and tied them there with strong cords. Then they pushed their heads down and shaved off all their hair.

"You're criminals!" the leader screamed. "Counterrevolutionaries! You have to pay for your crimes!" He gave the order to take my parents out. But they resisted, struggling. For this their faces were beaten bloody with belts . . . . I saw blood running from their mouths.

A final plea, one last effort. My grandparents, Mimi and I grabbed the legs of these men to stop them from taking our parents away. But that was stupid. They began to beat us as if we were rabid dogs, crushing our hands under their enormous shoes.

We were overcome by pain, by humiliation. We crawled on our bellies, choking. I saw my parents swallowed up by a truck which vanished in a cloud of dust. I could hear them calling, "Niu-Niu! Mimi!" Then, after this nightmare of tears, blows, fire and blood, their voices too seemed to fade away into nothing.

The four of us stayed in the courtyard for a long time, dazed, staring into space. My grandparents were trembling like autumn leaves in a storm. Silent tears rolled down their cheeks. They muttered hoarsely, "My God, what's happened? What have we done to deserve such punishment?"

At last we turned back into what was left of our home. What destruction! Piles of charred books were still smoldering. The wind blowing through the tattered curtains stirred the grey cinders. Only smothered sobs broke the silence. My grandfather held his hands over his eyes, shaking his head. He could not grasp that the house was suddenly so filthy, so empty — devastated.

My grandmother, her arms around me, tried to console me. I realized then that tears tasted of salt.

My memories began on that day when I was four years old. Ten days after I was born, on May 16, 1966, the "Great Cultural Revolution" had erupted. From a haze of banners and ubiquitous posters, the Red Guards had emerged, harbingers of death. I am haunted to this day by nightmares from that time.

I could not understand why my parents had to leave, why their mouths were bleeding. Were they hurt? Where had they gone? Why had the house been ransacked?

 Chapter 2
MIMI

A few days after my parents left, "they" came back to search the house again. They chased us out as if we were animals. Apart from a few clothes and some dishes, we had lost everything.

They made us move into a disgusting, damp old shack. Cold rain trickled inside the walls; the wind blew through innumerable cracks. Even in this slum, we still had no peace. The neighbors put up posters covered with writing all over the outside walls of our shack and even on the door, and forced Grandpa to read them aloud. That must have been too much for him, because after dinner he started to go out and tear them all down; but Grandma stopped him, insisting that the posters protected us from the wind. "The house is too cold for the children," she said.

Grandpa must have noticed the look of hopeless fear in our eyes; his own became teary and red. It gave me a strange feeling to see him throw himself weeping into my grandmother's arms, like a child who has been punished unfairly. Mimi went up to him and pulled gently at his sleeve. "Grandpa, don't cry. We're warm, we're really warm. We really are."

I think that those words just added to his bitterness. He panted with exertion as he lifted my big sister up in his arms. "Mimi, my grandchild, I'm not crying. I'm glad you're so understanding."

Somehow in this cold, bare place we had to sleep. The four of us huddled together for warmth on a wooden platform supported by bricks, that served as our bed. The night seemed long to me. I was filled with a new emotion: I no longer believed in my lucky star. Everything could change: from one day to the next, people could suddenly be hungry, in rags, and a child could lose her parents. I was afraid of what tomorrow might bring.

Some days later, Mimi was looking at photos of our parents while she was writing. Her tears fell softly on the paper.

"What are you writing, big sister? Why are you crying?"

"I'm writing them a letter. It's been so long since they left. I'm asking them to come back right away."

"Where have they gone? How will they get the letter?"

"I don't know, Niu-Niu. I think you just put the letter in the mailbox. That's what I've seen grown-ups do."

Her envelope had no address.

I asked her to write a letter for me. I needed them so much.

"Don't cry, Niu-Niu. Don't cry, little sister." She stroked my hair, but she was weeping harder than I was.

Mimi often took care of me. On one occasion she gave me her red hair ribbon, on another, a flowered handkerchief. . . the little that she had. She kept telling me that Papa and Mama would come back soon. But they still hadn't come when Mimi herself went away.

It was getting very dark. My big sister should have been back from school. We began to worry and went out to look for her. We found her at last cowering in a corner of her classroom, her hair disheveled, her face scratched, her clothes torn, the contents of her schoolbag scattered everywhere. She was sobbing.

Grandpa spoke to her softly, "What happened? What are you doing here?"

She looked up at us as if she were seeing angels. She cried out and threw herself into my grandfather's arms.

He understood. There was nothing to say. He kept his arm tight about her while we walked silently back to our shack.

"Grandpa, I don't want to go back to school. I want to see Papa and Mama again. I'm scared, I'm so scared . . . ." With each word Mimi's whole body trembled. Grandmother washed her face and combed her hair, hoping to make her feel better.

"They threw stones at me, they spat in my face, they pulled my hair, they tore up all my notebooks and they threw my schoolbag into the mud. They said terrible things about you, Grandpa and Grandma, and they said terrible things about Papa and Mama. And when I went to the professor, he said that it was my fault that I was your granddaughter, that I deserved what they did to me. I don't want to go back! I don't want to be your grandchild any more!"

Her harsh and bitter words stung my grandmother. Grandpa shook his head, trying to think of something soothing to say. He said he knew that Mimi was a good girl; he and Grandma loved her very much. Those others were the ones who were at fault. They were the ones who were mean and cruel. He told Mimi not to cry; she wouldn't have to go to school tomorrow.

But Mimi could not stop. "What did my parents do?" she cried. "Why do people treat us like this?"

My grandparents had reached the limit of their strength. For a long time, we all clung together.

Two days later I woke up suddenly in the middle of a stormy night to see my grandparents packing a large bag. A woman whom I didn't recognize was standing next to them. My big sister, dressed in her good clothes, was crying with her head bent. I heard Grandpa say to her, "We'll see you soon, Mimi. You'll go with this nice lady to the country. Darling, you know that you can't stay here any more. There you'll be able to attend school and no one will insult you any more. Everyone will be nice to you. I'm sure of it."

"Don't make me go! Papa and Mama are already gone; don't make me go too!"

"We're not abandoning you. We love you very much; we're going to visit you soon. That's a promise."

For me it was like a clap of thunder. Mimi was going away; it had to be my fault. I leapt up, throwing off my covers.

"Mimi, don't go! Don't leave me! I'll give you back your hair ribbon! And I won't cry so much, I'll do everything you tell me!"

She ran to me and caught me in her arms. "Don't send me away," she begged. "Niu-Niu and me, we'll be good, we promise! I'll go back to school tomorrow and I won't whine even if they hit me, even when it hurts! I'm not afraid of anything any more except losing you . . . ."

That was too much for our grandfather. Tenderly, he stroked Mimi's cheek with his emaciated hand, trying desperately to reassure her.

"How will I find the courage to let you go? I feel as though I'm being torn apart. It's even worse than that — but believe me, Mimi, you must go for your own sake, to protect your future."

Mimi understood, and, clinging to the hope of an early visit from us, she finally accepted the fact that she had to go.

She gave me her small pencil and I gave her back her red ribbon. I promised to save some candies, just for her. Then Mimi vanished into the pouring rain.

She surely could not have imagined for one moment that she was seeing Grandpa for the last time.

Chapter 3
NOURISHED WITH BLOOD

I have forgotten when my grandfather had to start working so hard. He had to get up long before dawn to sweep the street and move the garbage cans. Once he finished his job, they made him carry heavy stones from one place to another. There was no point to it but to humiliate and exhaust him.

He became a veritable beast of burden from morning to night, all the while wearing a kind of harness that cut into his emaciated body. Thus weighed down, he amused passersby who showered him with insults. As soon as he dragged his feet or even sighed, the Red Guards whipped him with their heavy-buckled belts. Never allowed to utter one word in his own defense, Grandpa endured the torment, while his tormentors kept on insulting him and beating him.

Grandma tried to help him bear the burden of the stones and the anguish. She was bitterly ashamed, but she made a strong effort to stop my grandfather from answering back. She begged the Red Guards not to beat him, to leave him alone. She forced herself to say that our family had done wrong, that we really were criminals . . . .

They laughed at her, "Not even a thousand deaths could make up for crimes like yours. Although we'll help you die anyway . . . ."

Just to get a little bit of respite, my grandmother agreed that everything the Guards said and did was right. Gradually their tormentors let it drop. Oh, yes, it's true that the Red Guards used every means to "aid" my grandparents.

Every day they forced my grandfather to do the same job over again. Every day except Saturday: that was different. Then both my grandparents would return with bruised, swollen faces and bloodied lips. At night I noticed black and blue marks on their bodies. I could not imagine what this special Saturday work was; my grandmother locked me in the house so that I would not find out.

I had to know. One Saturday I climbed out of the window and went outside to watch. I saw my grandparents on a kind of platform. They were bent over, hands behind their backs. A heavy iron placard was hung around their necks by a chain that forced them into an even more awkward position. Behind them were the colored posters of Mao Zedung that were to be seen everywhere at that time. "Long Live Mao," was on the left, "Glory to Mao," on the right and "Let Us Pursue the Cultural Revolution to the End!" on top. On the side was another poster, "Let Us Criticize and Annihilate that Terrible Criminal, Liu T'ai-Lung" — my grandfather — on the other side was a poster naming my grandmother.

The meeting had attracted three to four hundred people, all neatly dressed with their little portraits of Mao pinned to their jackets and their Little Red Books grasped tightly in their hands. They sang a hymn to the glory of Mao and then shouted in unison, "Long Live Mao! Long Live Communism!" The meeting could now start.

Speaker after speaker succeeded each other, seemingly never at a loss for words. I did not learn until later that all their speeches were denunciations of my grandparents.

A man who appeared to be a leader approached the microphone, waving a cane and a white shirt stained with red. "Comrades!" he shouted. "This shirt is proof of one worker's death under the bloody cane of Liu T'ai-Lung, who demanded back the yuan he had lent out. This swine killed one of your comrades. Have we the right to ignore this terrible crime?"

"No, we can't ignore it!" the spectators shouted in unison.

"Comrades, have we the right to let this cruel killer live?"

"No, we cannot let him live!"

Then, like automatons, they all shouted together, "Let's criticize and annihilate this terrible criminal, Liu T'ai-Lung and his wife!" The purpose of this incessant bellowing that filled heaven and earth was to force my grandparents once again to confess their errors and their worthlessness and to demand their own deaths. Yet they remained silent. All the fabricated evidence and these hateful lies left them mute, but they paid for their silence and their innocence with more violent blows to the face.

So this was the work they did on Saturdays! Paralyzed by horror at this ghastly game, but with my eyes now wide open, I witnessed clearly what to me was more unspeakable than a thousand deaths. I didn't want my grandparents to submit to this. I wanted to — I felt I *had* to — help them somehow. I called out to them to go back to the house. Stiffly like a little puppet, my heart beating, I walked up to the edge of the platform.

"Grandma, Grandpa, what are you doing here? Let's go back to the house!"

My words halted the stream of denunciation. The eyes of the chief accuser rapidly searched the audience. Finally locating the sacrilegious voice, he shouted, "Bring me this insolent little bitch!"

I felt large hands lift me, pushing me up onto the platform. The accuser appealed to his audience as witnesses. "Comrades, look at this child of criminals! At her age she already opposes the Revolution and the Party. As the great Mao has said, 'The offspring of a dragon is another dragon; the offspring of a Phoenix is another Phoenix.' And 'A mouse is born able to dig a hole in the wall.' This child of criminals has been fed on the blood of the workers."

None of this made sense to me. Everything was turning before my eyes. I called on my grandma for help. She went crazy, like a mother who has suddenly lost her child. Her large eyes were red with anger. It was as though time and space dissolved. Nothing could stop her. She cried out, "Niu-Niu! No, don't hurt her! She's still a baby! Yes, we've made mistakes! Yes, we ought to die! But *she* hasn't done anything! Don't hurt a mere child!"

She slipped and fell painfully against her placard. Immediately covered with blood, she crawled desperately toward me, evading those who sought to stop and beat her. I saw her bleeding and suddenly I stopped crying. I was no longer afraid; a blinding hatred came over me. With all my strength I bit the large hand holding me. That must have hurt. Blows rained down on me, but I no longer felt that kind of pain. By not fighting back I was able to escape, flying like a freed bird toward my grandmother.

"Grandma, you're all bloody! Your head is all red!"

Blood, dark red blood, the kind I'd seen too much of: the bloodied mouths of my parents when they were taken away, the blood that ran from my grandfather's nose when he came back in the evening; the blood on the scratched face of my big sister and here the blood that spurted from my grandma's head. So dark! How much more blood did my family have to spill for no reason?

My grandmother held me tightly to her. She dabbed at

the blood and tears on my face. "My little Niu-Niu, don't cry," she stammered. "I'm here with you, as always."

Then the others surrounded us, trying to separate us. They beat us, pulled at us, but they couldn't pry away my grandmother's arms. We were welded together by an invisible force. My grandma held me with almost supernatural strength.

If, as they had claimed, I had been nourished with blood, it was her blood, drop by drop, that had sustained me. It was she who had endured the shame and the poverty so that I might survive. I had drawn my very breath from her energy. And it was as though with each step that I had taken I had stepped on her body. No, they could never separate us!

They gave in, but not without further denunciation.

"With criminals like that, you can't go easy. From now on, no one will be permitted to help them, anyone who helps them will be treated as a criminal! Now let's go back to our session of self-criticism. Old or young, what's the difference! We'll criticize them all together!"

But Heaven did not cooperate. It poured its anger on our tormentors. A thunderstorm forced the crowd to disperse, leaving us alone. We rejoined my grandfather, still tangled in his bonds and black and blue from the beatings.

I hugged my grandma. "Grandma dearest, forgive me. I disobeyed. I left the house. It's all my fault . . . . But I didn't want you to die. I love you so much . . . . Does it hurt, Grandma dearest?"

"Niu-Niu, it's not your fault. It's because of our family. Forgive us. You're so young. Don't hate us!"

"I'd never do that!" All I wanted was to stop her bleeding. I was afraid of red, I was so afraid . . . .

The rain came down in sheets, the thunder sounded very

close. My grandmother freed Grandfather from the metal placard and picked me up in her arms. The three of us walked down the rain-drenched street to our house.

Chapter 4

A MODEL
REVOLUTIONARY

Rice had disappeared from our table long ago and it was some time since we had tasted even feed corn. For weeks and months all we had for our one meal a day was a mash of old potatoes, turnips and rice bran.

I finally got so sick of this mash that I could no longer touch it. My grandmother patiently assured me that if I ate the mash I would grow up to be very pretty. Of course I wanted to be pretty, so I ate it. I was convinced I was ugly because I had no friends at that time. When they saw me, all the children either fled or yelled insults at me.

One day I was playing with a little boy on a big sandpile. We were having fun throwing it around. Because I was still young and awkward, I threw some sand in his eyes. His mother, who had been sitting near us, came running up in a rage and began to scold her son, reminding him over and over again that she had absolutely forbidden him to play with me.

"Why didn't you obey me? You see how nasty she is! She threw the sand in your eyes. She's mean because she's the child of criminals. Now let's go!"

My little companion didn't want to leave; we were having fun. He said it wasn't my fault. But it was as if she were deaf. She walked off with long, determined strides, pulling him after her. The little boy looked back at me, sad and helpless. It made me so unhappy to lose my only playmate that I followed close behind them, catching hold of her skirt. "Please let him play with me, Ma'am. I'm not mean. I won't be nasty any more. I won't throw any more sand at him."

With a furious look, she shrieked, "Scram, little bitch! You disgust us!"

I went back to the sandpile by myself. My eyes filled with tears that also filled my heart before they dripped down on the sand. I realized what a mangy dog I was, one of those mangy dogs everyone hates.

My grandmother came to me and tried to comfort me.

"Come on, let's go home. I want my little Niu-Niu, she's the nicest little girl in the world. I'll play with you at home." But it wasn't any fun at home because I didn't have any friends. That was all there was to it.

My grandmother began to teach me to read and write and especially to recite some classical poems. Very soon I knew one by heart, repeating it endlessly. My grandfather was surprised and delighted listening to me. One evening he said to me, "Niu-Niu, if your parents could hear you, they would certainly be proud. Recite it once more for them."

Could they hear me over there, wherever they were? Could they see us? I had searched the sky in vain; there were no stars. Still, in the depth of the darkness, I could see my Papa and Mama whispering to me, "Recite your poem for us."

> Behind the window
> The moon's radiance
> Seems to frost the earth.
> I lift my eyes toward the moon,
> Then bow my head
> Thinking of my parents.

I added two lines of my own.

> Papa, Mama, come back soon.
> I miss you so!

I hated to see children walking with their parents on the street. It made me unbearably jealous. To my anguished questions, my grandma said that Papa and Mama were working far away and would come back some day. Some day! How could I know then that they would be gone for eight long years!

"His name was Chang Ta Pao which means 'big firecracker,'" Grandmother said. "He was a peasant's son who couldn't read or write, but he could really talk. Before the Cultural Revolution he had been a barber. One fine day he accidentally nicked his boss's ear while he was cutting her hair. He was sacked on the spot and then had to work as a streetsweeper to earn his living. But when the Cultural Revolution began, he became the head of a group of Red Guards. In fact, he destroyed his old boss's house just the way ours was wrecked. For the first time in his life he was top dog, a leader of men. He owed all this to the man who had sparked the Revolution, the great Mao Zedung. He adored Mao as if he were a god, much more than he had ever loved his own parents."

At the time that my grandmother told me this story, Chang Ta Pao was at the height of his power. I recognized him from the day that my parents were taken away and had seen him again at my grandparents' self-criticism session on Saturday. It was he who had been the little barber. His face

was to be more deeply etched in my memory as a result of
yet another demonstration — a mass meeting in honor of Mao
which we had been ordered to attend.

It was a beautiful day. Everyone stood dressed in his or her
best, solemnly waiting for the ceremony to begin. Finally, after a long delay, they all turned their heads toward a man
who was slowly mounting the steps to the platform.

"That's Chang Ta Pao," murmured my grandmother.

He wore an army cap, a handsome white shirt, khaki
pants, and was holding something wrapped in red paper.
Slowly he approached Mao's portrait and prostrated himself
in front of it several times before he turned to the audience.

"Comrades! Today I am going to do something special to
prove that my heart belongs to Mao. Comrades! Before the
Liberation, I was miserable. It's Mao and the Communist Party that saved me. Yet even then the criminals and capitalists
continued to harass me . . . . With the Cultural Revolution,
Mao saved me for the second time. All that I have today, Mao
gave me. That's why I swear before Heaven that I will give
every drop of my blood for Mao . . . ." Short of breath, he was
unable to continue, his eyes welling with tears. He was really
crying!

Carefully, he unfolded the paper to reveal a large pin with
the image of Mao on it. Suddenly, he became nervous. Then,
opening his shirt, he bared his chest. The silence was so intense that a cough from someone in the audience was like
a clap of thunder. His little fingers trembled feverishly as
he held the sacred object. He turned his back again and bow-
ing deeply before Mao's poster, addressed it. "Mao, you are
like a god to me and I will do all in my power to please you.
Accept the prayer of your humble servant." Saying this, he
turned around and before our disconcerted eyes, he pierced

himself with the pin of the medallion, pinning it to his chest. It was astounding!

Seeing his convulsed face turn white made one feel sick, as if the pin had entered one's own flesh.

A woman began to cry out, but she stopped under the pained yet stern gaze of Chang Ta Pao. He was sweating profusely, but bleeding very little. Suddenly, the crowd began to react with spirited applause, shouting, "Long live Mao Zedung. Let's follow the example of Chang Ta Pao!"

He wanted to smile, but he could only grimace from the pain. Later I learned from my grandfather that Chang Ta Pao had to go to Emergency because of the infection. The doctor who removed the pin was treated as a criminal: Chang Ta Pao would have preferred to die rather than to be separated from the medallion. Even though no one in the hospital dared to speak to him, he had to be cared for. Because he was acclaimed by the populace as a model revolutionary, to let him die would have been to risk one's own life. Finally, the problem was resolved with shots and medicines.

I saw Chang Ta Pao for the last time two or three months later. He had changed. One would have said he was a ghost, he was so thin and dirty. What was he doing carrying heavy stones along with my grandfather? He too was being beaten with belts. I couldn't believe my eyes. Nevertheless, it was he. Somewhat afraid, I quietly approached him. Curiosity overcame my fear and I asked, "Why are *you* here? Don't you go to the meetings any more?"

With a slow, lizard-like movement he turned toward me. His face became sinister and dark. He recognized me and began to shout like a madman, "Get out of here, daughter of criminals! I am not like you. *I'm* not a criminal!" His greenish face trembled. Suddenly, he fell to his knees, imploring

Heaven in a sombre, throbbing voice, "Mao, Mao, Mao, you know I adore you. My heart, my blood belong to you. Pardon me, for I have sinned. I deserve death because I misspoke. I must go to hell. Order your punishment . . . but please don't leave me with criminals. I'm ashamed and I have to die . . . I'm ashamed . . . I have to die . . . ."

Bending down as though in prayer, he kept striking his forehead on the ground until the guards rushed up and forced him with their straps to go back to the drudgery of carrying large stones. Watching him sadly shuffling off, I no longer felt hatred, but only pity.

When I asked my grandmother how Chang Ta Pao had become a criminal, she told me that in the middle of a meeting he had shouted, "For the love of President Mao, I decided to name my newborn son Mao Zedung!" No one could believe his ears. Hundreds of pairs of eyes stared at him with contempt. A second later there was a general outcry, "Down with Chang Ta Pao who brought such shame on Mao! Chang Ta Pao is a criminal! Let's get rid of him!" Before the wretch had time to understand his error, his hands were tied behind his back and he was savagely beaten.

My grandmother added, "He's an illiterate peasant. In China one shouldn't even pronounce the name of the emperor. How could he dare to give that name to his no-account son?"

Chang Ta Pao died a little while later. Like other gawkers, I went to see his body in the shack where his family had been "relocated" just as ours had been. I was still very young and horrified by the spectacle. The dead man was on his knees, his head on his chest. He had pierced his torso with another medallion of Mao. A piece of paper on his thigh read, "Forgive me, Mao." A fragment of his bloody tongue was sticking to the paper. He had slit his wrists with a kitchen knife and cut off his guilty tongue.

He left behind a son not yet a year old who was already branded a criminal. It seemed to me that life was becoming a farce. This could happen to anyone! One day you were a role model, the next day you were shouted down! First executioner, then suddenly, victim.

Later I saw a woman in rags, a baby on her back, crouching on the main square amidst half-burned charcoal debris. She no longer seemed to have a soul. If she had not been muttering, I would have taken her for a corpse. Her baby wept and cried out, but the passersby paid no attention. She was the widow of Chang Ta Pao. His family went on paying for his crimes. The poor woman had gone mad and wandered around the whole day, yelling. Then one day, she and her baby were no longer there. Was the baby still alive or left to die like an abandoned puppy?

I asked Grandmother what the poor woman was muttering about in the midst of the coals.

"She was reciting from Mao's Little Red Book."

Chapter 5
THE TIGER'S RUMP

Time was passing slowly and seemed somehow out of order: I was now five years old. May sixth, which is my birthday, is the beginning of summer in my part of China.

My grandma carried me in her arms to an old temple destroyed by the Red Guards. Of course, it was forbidden to come near it. However, in the bronze cauldron a few sticks of incense testified to the defiance of the faithful. The place was desolate and overgrown with weeds. My grandpa was already there, dressed in the traditional long robe of the educated. With a bouquet in his left hand, he was obviously waiting for us. Smiling, he came towards us and explained to my grandma, who was deeply touched, that he had not forgotten what day it was. Offering me the bouquet, he said that he had come to ask Buddha to look out for my future.

"Niu-Niu, today's your birthday. You're five years old and a big girl. I have only this bouquet of wild flowers to offer to you. Happy birthday, my darling! I hope that you become as beautiful as these flowers."

Holding hands, the three of us entered the temple. We burned the make-believe paper money that we had made at home, lit sticks of incense, then knelt before Buddha to pray. My grandpa told me I had been born under the sign of the Fiery Horse. "It's a good star, but often those who are born under it must endure a difficult youth. Now you have only a few flowers as your present, but I'm sure that when you're grown, you'll receive roses every day."

My grandma couldn't help but tease Grandpa for his flight of fancy. Naive as I was, I asked my grandmother just when I would see those beautiful days. "Later, no doubt, but don't expect them too soon." I would have to study hard, learn other poems and work diligently.

"If I write a hundred characters a day, will that be enough?"

My grandparents burst out laughing, "That will be quite enough."

When we got back to the house, I had the pleasure of a priceless gift from my grandmother — a hard-boiled egg! It really was a day of surprises.

I began to study with a new intensity to hasten that wonderful time when I would get roses every day. But life remained as it had been, dreary and leaden; each day we seemed to sink a little more deeply into the swamp of shame, cold and poverty.

Grandpa's pittance of a salary was hardly enough for the three of us to survive on. I found him oddly changed. Sometimes, with an absent smile, he would mumble the poems that I was reciting. More often, he was both depressed and irritable. What was he thinking of? Yes, Grandpa had changed a lot. He had been tall and robust; now he was bent and feeble. He talked less and less and became increasingly morose. And now he would also lose his temper with my grandmother: "The food is terrible! I just can't swallow this garbage any more!" He would get angry seeing our daily meal on the table, but my grandmother knew how to appeal to his feelings. "Look, Niu-

Niu has an appetite. She likes it!" He let himself be persuaded, but immediately put down his chopsticks again. "T'ai-Lung, you have to eat," she urged him. "You work so hard. Think of your health!"

"What health? They've taken all the fat from my flesh. There's nothing left to wait for but death."

Grandpa talked more and more about death, something that I could not yet fully imagine. One night in bed I overheard a conversation between my grandparents. Grandma had decided to scavenge for paper to help buy better food. She knew some old women who were doing that with their kids, but my grandfather would have no part of it. Not only did he think I was too young to carry the paper, but he refused to be dishonored before our ancestors. So on all counts, it was no: Grandma was not to do it!

Our house was really empty. In the one room, thirteen by sixteen, there were only a crude table and three chairs and a poor excuse for a bed. We had no mattress, only old newspapers and dried leaves to soften the wooden platform. Cotton filling escaped from the torn coverlet. The rickety table lacked a drawer and its top was falling apart. We kept our clothes on a shelf that we had put together with bricks and boards. In a bowl covered with paper, my grandmother carefully kept a pork rind, which, since we had no cooking oil, was used as the fat for our meals.

Our shack had two doors, one opening on the street, the other on a court in the back where my grandfather had built an oven of sand and stone. You could leave the doors wide open; no thief would bother to come in. The place was too poor to attract even the wind.

One afternoon, while my grandfather was working and my grandmother had left to find something to eat, I was alone at home, looking through some comic books recovered from a garbage can. As usual, when my grandfather returned his face was red and swollen. He had been beaten again. He sat down on a chair, staring into space. Hadn't he heard my greeting? Didn't he want to talk to me? I thought he must be tired and didn't dare to disturb him. Suddenly he leapt up and began to pace back and forth, gesticulating like a puppet and talking strangely.

"What to do? . . . No, I can't . . . Not like that . . . But there's no other solution . . . Too bad . . . Too bad about everything . . . That'll be better . . . Yes, it's best like that . . ."

I watched him furtively, hoping to figure out his mood, but he turned around towards me, stared at me, shaking his head, before talking to himself again. This time it was clearer. "My son, where are you? Mimi, do you think of me? My wife, do you hate me?" He called on all the family members, imagining that he was talking to each one.

"Grandpa, you're crying . . . . Grandpa?"

I didn't want to see him like that. I knew I could reach him; he had heard me. He trembled. His face had never looked so bereft of hope. "Niu-Niu, my darling. Grandpa is going far away. I won't see you until you're both grown up, Mimi and you. Will you forget your Grandpa?"

"No, Grandpa, no! When I grow up I'll stay with you all the time."

"Remember everything I've taught you. Never forget to be good and kind and to love and respect your grandmother."

"Grandpa! Where are you going? I want to go with you." I knew he was holding back his tears. He was talking to me as though I weren't there.

"It's no place for children over there. It's dark and cold.

There are no flowers and there's no sunshine, but for me it will be peaceful." He was describing a place that he seemed to have visited before. I followed his gaze, but I couldn't see anything there.

"Niu-Niu, tell your grandmother I am very sorry I led her such a hard life, that in another life I'd offer her something better. Niu-Niu, let me look at you and hug you one last time . . . ."

His voice broke with a sob and he held me tightly in his arms. Pressed against his heart, I heard a muffled rattling sound that seemed to come from deep inside.

He let go of me, moved toward the table like an automaton, took the kitchen knife in his hand and then stopped. He frightened me. His skeleton-like silhouette made my blood run cold.

"Grandpa, what are you doing? Don't go away!"

He hadn't heard a thing. He was already a ghost as he left the house.

I must have called after him once more. No doubt I wept. I didn't know what to do . . . . Suddenly my grandmother appeared like an angel from Heaven.

"Grandma! Grandpa left . . . The knife . . . He said he felt sorry for you."

"Where did he go?"

I pointed. She screamed and flung herself out the door, dropping the miserable food she had scrounged. There was a terrible cry, followed by my grandma's tremulous, tearful voice. "No, don't do that!"

I ran like lightning. My grandfather lay on the ground limp as an old doll, with one bloody hand fluttering in the air. My grandma had caught hold of the hand holding the knife. He tried to thrash about, shouting like a madman. "Let me die, let me go, I can't stand it any more! I can't stand it any more!"

My grandmother seized the knife, throwing it as far away as she could. She held tightly to my grandfather's wrist to staunch the bleeding. "T'ai-Lung, why did you do this? How could you have the heart to leave us? Didn't you think of your son?"

"I know he'll never come back. He's dead. I want to go over there to look for him, to meet him. I want to leave . . . ."

Talking exhausted him. Letting his hands drop, he began to weep.

"T'ai-Lung, you have to live and keep your hopes up. Our son will come back, I'm sure of it. You have no right to abandon us. We have to remain together."

My grandfather was clinging to my grandmother's jacket. "I want my son. I want to go back to our old home. This is too much for me!"

I was frightened and at the same time I felt a terrible sadness. I hated not being able to help him. But most of all I hated those who had done this to him.

Somehow or other, we half-dragged, half-carried him to the house. Fortunately the cut was not too deep. The two of us had saved him in spite of himself — doctors, of course, were denied to us. We didn't dare let the neighbors know either; they would have accused my grandfather of secretly rebelling against the Revolution and they would have made him pay for it.

With a few shreds of cotton from our bed cover and our clothes, we made a bandage. The poor man was so exhausted he fell asleep immediately, but in his sleep that night he kept shouting and crying out. Grandmother watched over him, bathing his forehead with a moist cloth, waiting to offer him something to drink.

In this terrifying nocturnal stillness, lit by the yellow glow of the candles, my grandmother told me the history of our family.

"Long ago, we lived in another city. From my earliest child-hood, I had heard of your grandfather's family, a powerful clan that owned a bank, a salt factory and some land in town. My own family was comfortably off but had little more than their good name. My parents had enough money to lead the peaceful life of the educated class at that time. I was taught all the social graces: my sister and I filled our days at home with embroidering, playing the lute, writing the calligraphy of classical poetry and playing checkers.

"The first time I saw your grandfather was the day of his wedding to my older sister. What a celebration! I was attracted immediately by his elegance and good looks, but my up-bringing did not allow me to stare. I knew I would probably not see him again because in those days it was improper for a young girl to be seen on the street, and whenever my sister visited us she came without her husband. I never expected that when I next saw him it would be at my sister's funeral.

"She died in childbirth, together with her baby. At the funeral he and I never spoke a word to each other. I noticed that he looked very thin. A short time later he asked my par-ents for my hand — at that time it was customary for a man to marry his dead wife's sister. It was my parents who decided on this union, but deep inside me, I was delighted. I'm still grate-ful to them for having given me such a good husband — so handsome, so considerate, so kind. He never lost his temper with me, and he was never arrogant towards the servants — he helped them out financially whenever they needed it. He inherited the salt factory and the bank and ran them, but your grandfather didn't care that much for money, Niu-Niu.

"We lived in a large, traditional two-story house; it had an upturned roof covered with glazed tiles. There was a wide, lush garden in front that ran down to the Blue River below. It was a family residence: uncles, aunts and their families lived with us. Counting the servants, there were about seventy or eighty of us. It was always very lively.

"Then your father was born. Grandpa couldn't contain his joy at having a son and he shared his happiness — he gave everyone red envelopes with money in them and we drank lots of rice liquor to celebrate. We were happy, but the good times never last. The war broke out; the Communists came. Our friends fled to other countries with their families. But your grandfather could not bring himself to leave this country and tear our big family apart.

"The war ended in 1949 and China was declared liberated. In fact, at Liberation we had to surrender our bank to the People's Bank and give up the factory, as well as all our other property, to the new government. Only the house was left to us, but the servants were no longer allowed to work there. Your grandfather gave each of them some money. I could not stop grieving over that; to me they had always been members of the family. The young woman who had been my personal maid since the age of thirteen was like a sister to me — in fact, when my parents died, she wept as much as I did. I gave her some beautiful clothes, and we stayed in touch. She wrote to me the day she married your grandpa's former chauffeur. She was the one who came to take Mimi to a safe place in the country. She's really a lovely person! I can never repay her for all her kindness and devotion.

"Niu-Niu, when you're grown up, remember to go see her, and tell her of my deep affection, my very humble gratitude . . . .

"Your father took it into his head to become an actor. For us, this seemed shameful — he should have been a banker to carry on the family tradition.

"That's how your grandfather and I came to move to this city, where your father had his professional start. It was around that time that our problems really began. The government forced us to write letters declaring how much money we had, how many servants and employees worked for us, whether we had ever killed anyone and whether we were still in contact with friends who had left China. Each detail was carefully checked. The fact that your grandfather had had two wives made matters worse. New sworn statements, new inquiries, new interrogations. Finally, everything seemed to return to normal.

"Our new house was the home that you knew so well: five rooms around a square inner court, just off a small street. The first thing Grandpa did was to set up a room for his last treasures: his library, art books and old paintings. The next room became the living room, where we took our tea and played mahjong. We made sure we hid our ancestors' altar, we camouflaged it in our bedroom, because the government forbade prayers to God. That didn't stop us from burning incense for the two little Buddhas that I loved so much.

"Your father turned out to be a good actor in the modern theater — that soon became the socialist theater. A little while after we moved here he met your mother. I didn't think she was very pretty, but she was certainly intelligent. Anyway, parents no longer have any say-so and he decided to marry her. Little by little, I discovered how really nice she was. She's a very fine actress, too, but sometimes I thought she was too jealous. One day when she was home alone, she burned all your father's fan mail. But they really loved each other passionately.

"Your grandfather was a salaried director in a government bank. He worked every day, and I took care of the house and looked after Mimi.

"In May 1966, the family was all excited waiting for you to be born, because the doctors said you were going to be a boy. We were all counting on that. Your grandfather was the happiest of us all; he asked me to make a fur-lined coat out of a tiger skin I had. He claimed that a boy who wore a tiger skin from his earliest days would grow up tall and handsome. What nonsense! I cut up my tiger skin for nothing! What a disappointment that you were only a girl!

"That day you really played a joke on us. That's why we called you 'Niu-Niu' — 'ill-natured.' Your grandfather didn't smile for days. But then you turned out to be so sweet; you weren't bad-tempered at all. You charmed people on the street. Grandpa said that this was because you were so proud of the joke you played on us. It was a good idea to give you this little name.

"As soon as you could walk, you were full of mischief. Once when your father was in a new play at the theater, before anyone noticed, you went up on the stage to talk to him. I'll never forget it. You said to him, 'Papa, this woman is not your mother. Grandma is sitting back there in the audience.' What a mess! Your father had some problems with the theater administration on account of it.

"Ah, it's true, my poor Niu-Niu, you were not born at a good time. Not only were you not a boy, but on top of that, the Cultural Revolution began ten days after you were born. The Red Guards began to kill the 'intellectuals.' Mao said he was a Red Guard himself; he set a percentage — three to five percent of those who were to be found guilty of 'revisionism.' They said they were fighting against what they called the four outmoded ways: 'old culture, old customs, old habits, and old ways of thinking.' They even changed the names of streets. Now each of their heroes has a boulevard named after him. They changed old-fashioned names for places of business — restaurants used to be called things like 'The Best Taste;' florist's shops were called 'Delicate and Subtle Fragrances.' Now they're all called things like 'Triumph of the Revolution.' — all you see in shop windows are large portraits of Mao. It used to be different. There were streamers all over — a kind you don't see any more. All these *dazibaos* — wall posters — what a waste! All that paper, ink and paintbrushes . . . .

"Your parents and their friends decided to write articles and post them in public to present their point of view. That caused them a lot of grief — as if they had touched the rump of the tiger, they had roused the wild beast. Their subversive opinions and our family's past were enough to make us criminals and counterrevolutionaries. You know what happened then . . . .

"But it's important that you know, Niu-Niu, that your family was always honorable. We've never lied. We were accused of murder, of keeping in touch with relatives who fled abroad and so forth. We thought that they were finished with us after the Liberation, but they never give up.

"You're terribly young, Niu-Niu, and I don't know if you understand everything that I've told you, but you must remember that when they torment us this way, when they push your grandfather to the brink, they do it out of malice, pure and simple. We've never been criminals. Don't hate us. You must respect your parents as much as they love you. We've always been honest and we've always told the truth. . . ."

My grandmother talked on until the candle burned down. In spite of the late hour, I didn't feel tired at all. I didn't quite understand everything she said, but I remembered all of it. Grandma warned me never to let anyone know what she had told me, or else things would get worse for us.

The sun rose at the cry of the rooster and once again the world stirred to life. I felt that I had grown up in one night. From then on, I was warmed by a great hope: I wanted to become an adult so that I could know everything and help my grandparents. I thought I could find a way to bring my parents back. Ten thousand questions whirled around in my head. The first: why did I have to wait to grow up?

Chapter 6
FLESH AND BONE

My grandfather was sweating profusely from the fever. It was almost noon and he still wasn't awake. My grandmother, ever solicitous, was going out of her mind trying to find something useful to do. I took out the last bowl of dry rice that we had put aside with such difficulty. The rice had become dirty over time, so I washed it carefully. Then I decided to add the precious pork rind to make a soup that would be more nourishing for Grandpa. It smelled so good my stomach growled, but I couldn't eat any of the soup that was meant for him. He was so feeble. Finally he woke up and looked at us through glassy eyes. He was breathing slowly, carefully, as if each breath would be his last. Then he said, "Why did you let me live? Why?" He called my grandmother by her nickname, Qing-Qing. "I've behaved so badly toward you these last few days . . . Why didn't you reproach me?"

She placed her hand tenderly on his mouth and whispered in a trembling voice, "T'ai-Lung, I will stay with you forever — I'll be at your side whatever happens, that is my choice. We must stay together till our son comes back. Don't leave me alone. I need you."

With his emaciated hands, he dried her tears, nodding his head.

I took the soup off the fire and handed it to Grandpa, urging him to eat every bit of it to get his strength back. He smiled with difficulty. He was too weak to hold the bowl, so my grandmother fed him spoonful by spoonful. The two of them made a peaceful, touching picture. At that moment I could almost see the robust, smiling Grandfather she had described to me. As he slowly ate the gruel, I wished over and over that he would recover and that our lost happiness would be restored.

Suddenly there was a loud banging at the door. My grandmother opened it and was shocked to find herself facing a band of Red Guards. Their leader glanced around the room; his eyes focused on the bowl of soup.

"Well!" he said bitterly. "So now you're dining in bed, are you?"

This made my grandmother very nervous. "Comrade, my husband is sick. He has a high fever and he can't get up!"

"Sick! He doesn't look sick to me. But even if he's dying, he has to go to work!"

My grandpa stared at him with loathing. He gathered all his strength to stand up and speak, taking a quick breath after each word. "You're men with wolves' hearts and dogs' lungs. You kill and burn everything in your path. Aren't you afraid of going to hell?" He gasped for breath. "You are destroying the Chinese people, you are trying to separate those who are as united as flesh and bone. Aren't you afraid of leaving nothing behind?"

My terrified grandmother rushed to his side to stop him from saying anything else, but it was too late. The Red Guard had lost face. He turned red, and sputtered, "Who do you think you are? You don't scare me . . . ."

He suddenly kicked over the table, spilling the precious soup on the dirt floor. The stage was set for tragedy. My grandfather was beside himself with rage.

"You're nothing but a filthy beast fit for slaughter!" He butted his head into the brute's belly, knocking the wind out of him. Then he spat in his face. The guard shouted, "Kill him!" and seized a rifle from one of the others. With all his strength, he began to strike my grandfather on the lower back with the butt, as if he were trying to cut him in two. My grandfather rolled on the ground, while the other guards hit him with everything within their reach, beating him savagely on the head, the legs, the arms. They were the claws and fangs of the militia leader.

My grandmother and I threw ourselves on the men. My grandmother, having lost her will to live, tried to absorb the blows. We both grabbed their legs. She begged them in God's name to spare Grandpa. But they pulled her hair and punched her viciously in the face. Little as I was, I did what I could. I bit one of the hands that was hurting my grandmother, digging my teeth in as deeply as I could, almost dislocating my jaws until the blows rained down on me, too.

"No, little Niu-Niu, not you!" We could see the whites of my grandfather's bloodstained eyes. Blood streamed from his mouth. He held out his hand, his whole body shivered. A gush of blood covered my grandmother; it reached me and sank into the earth floor.

Suddenly it was quiet. My grandmother turned away from the guards and with a cry that seemed to rend heaven and earth, fell upon my grandfather's inert body. Frantically, she tried to clean the blood that covered him. "Wake up, T'ai-Lung!" She caressed him, rocking him back and forth.

"You've killed him! T'ai-Lung, open your eyes, look at me once more. You can't die, you promised me . . . My T'ai-Lung . . . My God, if you have eyes to see, bring back my husband!"

She wept, holding on to his head which had been reduced to a bloody pulp: I clung to the corpse. "Don't leave, Grandpa. You haven't finished your soup. Your little Niu-Niu wants you to come back. Wake up, Grandpa!"

The Red Guards pulled us away from the body. Nothing could soften the hearts of these wolves. "Even if he's dead, he'll have to submit to a self-criticism session. We must continue the Cultural Revolution to the end! Take him away!"

Why should we continue to cry and howl? What was the point of clinging to Grandpa any longer? There was nothing left but a bloodstained rag. Was nothing left of his body, his spirit, his voice that had given me so much love and warmth? Where did you go, Grandpa, without saying good-bye, without holding my hand and without giving Grandma one last look? Are you cold or hungry over there where you are?

A few days after my grandfather's death, a man came to our house. Unfolding a letter, he began to read aloud in a solemn voice: "The counterrevolutionary, Liu T'ai-Lung, who scoffed at President Mao and the Communist Party despite the active effort of the people to reeducate him, persisting in his crimes, has recently proved his hostility to the Revolution by committing suicide. Today you are being officially notified of this."

They must have thought we were fools.

"No, he didn't commit suicide. You beat him to death! You killed him right before our eyes and then you stole his body!"

"You have to pay ten yuans for the cost of cremation," the man said woodenly. "The Party and the Government never pay these charges for a counterrevolutionary."

"Are you deaf? He didn't commit suicide! He wasn't a counterrevolutionary!" My grandmother was beside herself, but the messenger remained unmoved.

"Pay the ten yuans or you won't get the ashes."

That was the last straw. Not to give us the ashes! Why would *they* want them? It was a curse for us not to have them. From under the bed, my grandmother took out some change — our meagre savings — and offered them to the Red Guard.

"That's not enough. That's not ten yuans."

"What are you saying? When our son comes back, you'll get the rest. If our son doesn't return, our grandson will honor the debt. Our family will not be wiped out."

The man must have realized by the way she was ranting that he couldn't squeeze any more out of us. He left. No one came back and we got nothing. Had my grandfather's body really been left somewhere for the vultures? For a while, thinking about all this made my grandmother lose touch with reality. Waking from my nightly nightmares, I would find her sitting next to the one small window, talking softly to herself.

"T'ai-Lung, you're not coming back? Do you hate me for not letting you end it all yourself? Do you hold me responsible for your having to submit to this savagery? I'm unworthy of you. Because of me, you have neither ashes nor grave. I couldn't have imagined that . . . I beg your soul to forgive me . . . I'm unworthy of you . . . I'm a criminal . . . T'ai-Lung, are you listening?"

She rambled on like this for several days. Sometimes she woke me to tell me that she had seen him and that he had forgiven her. I was furious that she hadn't let me know in time because I wanted to know where he had gone and why he didn't come to see me too. She explained to me, "Your grandfather is dead. He lives on the moon now."

I was five years old. I had just learned that the death of someone dear is much more difficult to bear than humiliation or hunger.

 Chapter 7

BIG BROTHER, THE HUNCHBACK

From now on we lived only for each other. My grandmother had found herself some work to help us survive: she made matchboxes at home. In the mornings she searched garbage cans for old paper that she sold to a factory. My grandfather had forbidden this, but without the fifteen yuans that he had earned for his hard labor, we had no money. This was the first time my grandmother had ever gone against her husband's wishes.

When people noticed that she was no longer in her right mind, the meetings found other victims. But we were still being harassed by men and by children who followed us in the street, spitting, throwing stones at us and chanting, "Crazy old lady, crazy old lady, smelly old hag who drags around a little counterrevolutionary runt!"

My grandmother chose to ignore them as she rummaged through the garbage, but none of it escaped me. One day, one of these kids hit my grandmother in the face with a stone and they all laughed loudly. I flew at the brat, grabbed him by the collar and began hitting him furiously. "Leave my grandmother alone!"

My grandmother and I were both surprised by my strength. She ran up and pulled me away from them. "Niu-Niu, what are you doing?"

"He threw a stone at you! He hurt you!"

"No, it was nothing."

"One day when I'm grown up, I'll kill them all no matter how many there are!"

She stared at me with a look that I had never seen before. It made me turn cold with fear and I didn't dare to look her in the eye. But I didn't understand how I was at fault.

"Niu-Niu, did you forget what grandfather told you? You have to be a good person in spite of misfortune and suffering?" She begged me never to lose my temper again. Did we have the right to kill people? Had desperation made me so stupid? It seemed I had risked losing the love of the one person left to me in the world.

This was the beginning of another phase of my education. I watched my grandmother, whose every word, every gesture, every tear, taught me about life. She took me to work with her and in the evenings she taught me poems by candlelight. I learned how to make the matchboxes. She helped me wash myself as well as I could and deloused me every evening before I went to bed. We were always together, waking up at the same time and going through the day together.

Winter arrived, indifferent to the fact that we had nothing to keep us warm. What we earned gathering paper all went to buy rotting food. We scrounged in the trash from the factory to find charcoal. Every morning, holding me by the hand, her bamboo basket on her back, my grandmother went to search for pieces of usable charcoal. Behind the large building other kids dressed in rags like me, with disheveled hair and dirty faces, were playing happily on the black heap. I felt a kinship with them and I liked to come back every day. Of course, fights broke out regularly, because the stronger forced the weaker to surrender half of what they found. I kept myself at a good distance or else I'd come early in the morning to avoid the troublemakers. Often I had to run back to the house.

One day at dawn the place was deserted. I was carefully gathering my treasure when I found a pile that, strangely enough, had been abandoned. Someone must have forgotten it. I was putting it into my own basket when I heard a clear and delicate voice that sounded like a silver bell. "Brother, we have to go. Mama will wake up."

I looked up to see a girl of about twenty, so beautiful that she took my breath away. She was with a short, hunchbacked boy of about the same age. He was using his jacket to carry charcoal. At first he had been smiling at me, but as he approached, I did not have time to put back all the charcoal I had found. The boy shouted at me angrily, "Hey you! Why are you stealing our charcoal?"

I remained glued to the spot with fear until he came up to me and furiously emptied my basket. "If you're already stealing at your age, what will you be like when you're grown?" I felt my face grow hot. "I didn't steal it! I didn't see anyone, so I took it." He went on scolding me while he filled his basket.

Sputtering with indignation, I turned to the pretty girl. "I didn't steal! I come here every day too; I was scavenging by myself."

"I know her," she said to her brother. "She's the granddaughter of that crazy old woman. Her parents were actors, they were arrested . . . . Do you really come here every day? Where are your grandfather and grandmother?"

My grandfather. Why did she have to mention him? I suddenly saw him collapsed before my eyes. I wanted to run away as fast as I could, but her gentleness and her comforting voice made me want to answer.

"Grandma goes through the garbage cans and Grandpa is

living on the moon."

"On the moon?"

"Yes. Grandma told me that when people die, they go up there to watch over us." She took my hand and shook her head compassionately. Her brother's attitude changed too: he gently asked my name and age. "Niu-Niu, I'm sorry I was a little gruff." He emptied half his charcoal into my basket. "I saw your parents act in the theater. My sister and I really admired them. Your father was magnificent."

This was the first time a stranger had said anything good about my parents. These few compliments were worth all the gold in the world. Reassured by their kindness, I was suddenly afraid they might disappear on the spot and that I'd never see them again.

"Is it true that my parents were fine actors? You really saw them? What did they look like?" I asked so many questions in quick succession just to keep them there, questions that puzzled them more than anything else.

"You don't know what your parents look like? You've forgotten them already?"

I was ashamed, but I hadn't lied to them. It was such a long time since my parents had left. I could only defend myself by bursting into tears. "It's not my fault! I didn't want to forget them. I miss them every day!"

It warmed my heart when they offered to walk me back home. I noticed how terribly ugly the boy was; his deformed, hunchbacked body reminded me of a toad. He was like those demons in my grandfather's tales, but I couldn't help but find him likeable. He would soon become my brother. Holding his hand, I felt only three fingers. Shouldn't there be five? I was still musing about this additional handicap when we arrived home. My grandmother hadn't returned yet. Before leaving, my new friends promised to stop by for me next morning. From the doorstep I watched them as they left, and I thought about them all the rest of the day.

I was dying with impatience to tell my grandmother about my adventure as soon as she returned. Much to my surprise, she already knew the girl and her brother. "They call him the hunchback. No one knows his real name. His father has been dead a long time and his mother is bedridden. All three of them live on the boy's earnings. He lost two fingers as punishment for a theft. No one can help noticing how beautiful she is and how ugly he is."

After that they came by for me every morning to go charcoal-gathering with them. Despite the difference in our ages, they seemed like close friends. The girl's infinite goodness impressed me even more than her beauty and, after a while, I no longer found her brother ugly. A great love united them: they were always together. He was constantly picking flowers for her and, once in a while, he would stick a flower in my hair, too.

One day a white cat that she left with me for the night disappeared from our house. I finally found it in the arms of a tall boy who didn't want to give it back to me. "Tell Mei Lin to come look for it herself."

"But who is Mei Lin?"

"She's the monster's sister."

Mei Lin, whom I had simply called "my sister" as the hunchback did, had been watching from afar. Flushed with rage, she ran up to us and snatched the cat from his hands. "*You're* the monster! Bad luck to you and your filthy family!"

"You're really too pretty," the hoodlum answered her. "It's too bad you drag your brother around with you everywhere. That keeps us from having anything to do with you."

Looking even more regal in her anger, Mei Lin gritted her teeth, marched straight up to him and slapped him twice, as hard as she could.

As time went on, we became closer. My two friends came to visit my grandmother regularly. Even though Grandma no longer spoke much, they passed the time together, Mei Lin assembling matchboxes and her brother bundling the paper we had gathered. My constant chattering was the only sound during these visits.

But then for three weeks we did not hear from my two friends. Although they lived far away, I talked my grandmother into visiting them. When we arrived, Brother greeted us at the doorstep. I threw myself into his arms, asking a thousand questions. He had been sick, he said, and he offered me a potato, which quickly distracted me from my questions. Inside, we met my friends' mother, who was indeed bedridden. Mei Lin stood disconsolately next to the bed as her mother told my grandmother that Mei Lin might be sent to the countryside for reeducation; Party members claimed it was the law.

"You see, my good lady, that I'm an invalid. Mei Lin is the only one in the family in good health. How shall we manage if she leaves?"

But Brother had already thought of a plan to save his sister. He intended to have an X-ray taken of his hump and to claim that it was Mei Lin's. All this seemed very risky to me, but their talk interested me less than the potato that I was enjoying. When we got home I hardly noticed that my grandmother was uneasy.

A month went by without my friends coming to see me. Then one night, a tearful Mei Lin, terribly frightened, came knocking at our door. "Help me, I beg you. Do something for my brother!"

We urged her to tell us what was wrong. "I deserve something worse than death," she said, sobbing. "You remember that my brother had an X-ray taken in order to protect me . . . One day a member of the Party called me in to tell me that he was not blind to the fact that the X-ray was a fake. For a crime like that — trying to avoid the reeducation of young intellectuals in the countryside — the guilty person has to go to prison. So of course I fell on my knees, begging him to leave my brother alone. Finally he said he would study our case. He asked me to come back that evening for his answer. When I came back, he . . . he . . ."

Poor Mei Lin wept uncontrollably. With a terrible cry she threw herself into my grandmother's arms. My grandma seemed to know the rest of her story: she angrily cursed the Party official.

Mei Lin calmed down somewhat and went on. "He warned me not to tell anyone about what he had done. I agreed because I was terrified that he would punish my family. But my mother kept questioning me because I kept throwing up. Tonight she talked to my brother about it and I broke down and told them everything. How could I have known that he would hit me and then pick up a kitchen knife and dash out like a madman? When he came back a while later the knife was bloody and the Red Guards were on his heels and arrested him. I beg of you, Grandmother, help us! I don't know what to do."

This was certainly terrible, but what had the Party member done to make her brother attack him like that?

My grandmother, who had been boiling with helpless rage, suddenly had an idea: Mei Lin should stay at our place where those "bastards" would never think of looking for her. My grandmother would go and see what she could find out. I might be useful because they would never notice a little kid, so she took me along to the court of a lighted building. I was proud to be helping Big Brother, as if his safety depended on me. We had barely arrived when we were paralyzed by a dreadful scream. Instinctively, we clutched each other's hand, shivering with apprehension. My grandmother, after calming down, told me to inch my way quietly up to the half-open door.

"I think your Big Brother is being held in there, but above all, don't let them see you, don't make any noise! That would just make everything worse for him. Come back quickly to tell me what's going on. I know you're brave."

Now I was really afraid of what I was going to see, but my feelings for him pushed me forward. Through the half-open door, I saw what a real torture session was like. They had forced him to lie on his belly, stripped to the waist. On his back they had placed an overturned table weighed down with huge stones that a guard was pounding with a club. Five men, whips in hand, were circling him.

"Well, you've got guts, you piece of crap! You had the nerve to lie to Party members and you mocked the Revolution. You've even killed one of us! Now if you don't know who makes the law around here, we're going to teach you. First we'll flatten your hump. Then, whenever we feel like it, we'll finish you off! What do you say to that?"

Big Brother let out an inhuman cry as blood oozed out of the corner of his mouth. With my heart in my throat, I found myself next to my grandmother without knowing how I had got there.

"Crushing his hump?" She couldn't believe her ears. She thought I hadn't seen clearly. If only that were true!

When we returned home, we found that Mei Lin had left,

and we never saw her again. For the next few days, rumors spread about Big Brother: that he had died, that he was alive in prison, or that somehow he had escaped and was hiding in the countryside.

For a short while I expected to see the hunchback again. That whole family had been destroyed like a torn-up snapshot. Several evenings in succession we heard horrible cries echoing around their house. I told myself that it was perhaps the ghost of Big Brother, or Mei Lin, or her mother. In any case, it was someone's ghost who haunted the place, demanding justice. One day a light inside indicated that another family had moved in.

My life seemed to move in fits and starts. While the revolutionaries pursued their glorious march, the world around me had a way of bursting like a toy balloon. At the age of six, I could already take stock: everything was possible in this world of madmen. The dead and the living held hands; people feasted behind brightly lit windows, while others fought like dogs to keep from dying of hunger. On one side, there were those who laughed; on the other, those who wept. Where could one go if one could no longer laugh or cry?

Chapter 8
ONE JOYOUS DAY

I went back to the loneliness that was my lot as "a child of criminals." In my monotonous daily life which consisted of scavenging for charcoal, the only happy note was Mei Lin's little white cat. From time to time, my grandma and I would pick up discarded vegetable leaves from the ground at the market. In the evenings, when we weren't laboriously making matchboxes, we studied poems from the T'ang dynasty and other periods.

I walked alone on the streets where others were writing propaganda posters or marching under red flags. I was completely indifferent to the bustle of that world. When I found an apple core or some other leftover food, I cleaned it carefully, then wolfed it down with intense pleasure. It was all a matter of what you were used to.

One day in September, my grandmother came home smiling. This simple sign of contentment has stayed in my memory like some rare and precious relic. Because she had to carry the heavy bundles of paper, my grandmother, who was a short woman, had shrunk even more. Her hair had turned completely white and every day her lined face became more wrinkled. But that evening she took me on her lap, saying enthusiastically, "Niu-Niu, my baby, I haven't paid much attention to you lately and I've made your life miserable, but today I have a big surprise! Guess what?" Her eyes sparkled like stars and I felt excited myself.

"Oh, I know! Candy!" That was something she had promised me for a long time. She shook her head with an enigmatic smile. Was it possible that there was something better than sweets? Unless . . . but that was impossible! Fearfully I tried again, "Papa and Mama?" No, that wasn't it either. My face clouded over.

"Niu-Niu, after tomorrow you'll be like the other children." Two shining tears trickled down her cheeks. "You'll be able to go to school. Can you imagine? To go to school and get a real education? It's very important! I'm so happy. Do you understand how lucky you are?"

At the moment it didn't make the slightest difference to me, but I agreed just to make her feel good. In fact, the guessing game itself had given me more pleasure than the prospect of going to school. But when I thought about it, I really was glad. So, after tomorrow, I too would take my schoolbag and, all dressed up, proudly go to the school that up to now I had merely seen from the outside. And all this thanks to Grandma.

The night before the great day, working by candlelight, she made me an amazing patchwork schoolbag with pieces of cloth that she had found in trash cans.

"Niu-Niu, you must study as hard as you can and obey the teachers. Your teacher of Chinese has arranged for you to be allowed to go to school. She saw your parents perform in many plays. I'm sure she'll be very nice to you." With all this advice, I was full of good resolutions. Yes, I would really study, even more than I had to.

I couldn't sleep that night. I tried to imagine my school, the people I would meet there, the games we would play. And before falling asleep I imagined that my teacher looked just like Mei Lin.

I woke up before dawn, full of excitement, and slipped into special clothes that we saved for special days and holidays: going to the temple, my birthday, my father's birthday, and the anniversary of my grandfather's death when we burned incense and prayed before his tiny photograph. After each of these events, these clothes, mended in a thousand places but the only ones without holes, were folded and put away. In fact, the blue color was faded almost to white.

In my patchwork schoolbag that looked like a field of flowers I had a pencil with an eraser which cost five maos, the pen my sister Mimi had given me, a small notebook that I had made from salvaged paper, and a piece of steamed corn bread for my lunch. Under one arm I carried the stool that each schoolchild was supposed to bring. I clung to my grandmother with my other hand. We were on our way.

It was dawn; roosters were crowing. Aside from occasional milkwomen and sweepers, there wasn't even a cat in the empty street. The fresh breeze, the crunching of our feet on the leaves, the light of the street lamps and the warmth of my grandmother's hand filled my senses. Completely elated, I was thinking to myself, Grandma is really too good to me. I swear that when I grow up, I'll do all I can to take care of her, to see that she's happy.

At the corner of one of the deserted streets, we passed a wooden gateway which brought us to a square courtyard surrounded by long one-story buildings. We crossed the courtyard where children were playing and entered a classroom. A teacher was standing next to her desk waiting for us. Long braids fell to the waist of her blue uniform; she was a beautiful girl in her twenties. She turned toward me, friendly and gracious. It was as if the sun lit up the room.

"Here we are, Professor Yang," my grandmother said humbly as we approached.

"Your name's Niu-Niu, I believe. What a pretty name." It had been such a long time since anyone had smiled at me while saying my name that I was overwhelmed. Because I had lived such an isolated life, I didn't know how to address a stranger. Shyly I hid behind my grandmother.

"Come, Niu-Niu, say hello to Professor Yang. Thank her for accepting you in her class." Somewhat frightened, my throat dry, I obeyed in an almost inaudible voice. My grandmother took hold of my hand so we would both bow respectfully before our benefactress.

"Please rise. I'm only doing my duty. Don't worry, I'll watch over Niu-Niu."

My grandmother, filled with emotion and close to tears, seized hold of Professor Yang's hand and nodded her head vigorously as a sign of gratitude and respect.

"Niu-Niu," said Professor Yang, "you must study conscientiously at school to make your grandmother proud of you."

It was my turn to nod my head like a little goose.

Dear Professor Yang, who smiled at me when she called me by my name, who gave me love and unlimited devotion and who simply considered me a human being. I will never forget her.

In the classroom next door, where the students were already in their places, the teacher introduced me to my table partner. "Here's your new schoolmate. Her name is Niu-Niu. Take good care of her."

"Hi, my name is Chou Chiang."

Immediately I sensed that he was very nice. Well-dressed

and pleasant-looking, he seemed as shy as a girl. On the table in front of him was a pretty box of pencils and a brand-new notebook.

Professor Yang went back to her desk and greeted her small pupils, who rose and greeted her in return. She introduced me, encouraging them to welcome me with applause. I blushed to the roots of my hair, surprised to see myself suddenly treated like a princess in one of my grandmother's tales.

I was living a dream. I learned to write the numbers one to ten, and to write, "Long live Mao." I discovered that $1 + 1 = 2$ and $2 + 2 = 4$. More wonderful yet, Chou Chiang came to talk with me during recess. He found my bag very pretty and wanted to know where I had bought it. Very proudly I told him that my grandmother had made it. I also showed him the notebook that I had put together myself. He admired it and I was overcome when he asked me to make one for him in exchange for a pencil.

"Sure, we have plenty of paper at home. I could make a lot of them." His friendliness filled me with feverish joy. Afraid that I would ruin other moments like this, I refused the pencil he wanted to give me.

At lunchtime everyone took out food. A magical piece of white bread stuffed with meat appeared in my neighbor's hand. I swallowed hard, and ate my miserable piece of corn bread.

In the afternoon after gym class, there was a general assembly to mark the beginning of the year. Each teacher climbed on the podium installed in the courtyard and gave his ritual speech. I was impressed by how many teachers there were. Professor Yang was the school principal and taught us Chinese; another professor taught mathematics, another drawing and the last one was the gym instructor.

Finally, the students returned to their classes to elect three delegates: one to be charged with supervising the two other pupils who did the cleaning up, one to collect the daily home-work and the last one to announce the arrival of Professor Yang every morning, leading the others in singing out, "Good morning, Professor!" I was so excited by all these marvelous events that I did not vote. Just having had the opportunity to do it made me very happy.

At the end of the day, Professor Yang, who walked with me to the gate, reminded me to come early the next day because I had cleaning duty. She also wanted me to convey her re-spects to my grandmother. Even though I kept my eyes low-ered while repeating, "Thank you, Professor Yang," the happi-ness of this school day had left me in complete confusion. She tenderly stroked my hair, saying, "Don't be late, or your grandmother will be worried."

For a moment I stood in a daze, following her with my eyes until she disappeared into one of the buildings. With my heart leaping, I gaily skipped toward our house.

Grandma was leaning against the doorway waiting for me. I threw myself into her arms. "My little Niu-Niu, here you are, from now on you're a big girl. Going to school is fun, isn't it?" She took me inside; a dish with meat cooked especially for me was already on the table. "Eat well to please me and tell me all about school."

I was so hungry and the impressions were so jumbled in my head that I couldn't be coherent. All I could say was, "Every-thing was fine, everything went well."

Once my plate was clean, my silence gave way to a flood of words. "The lead in my pencil broke and when he saw how panicked I was, Chou Chiang let me use one of his pencils.

You wouldn't believe the lovely colored pencils, pretty pens and erasers in his box. He even has a pencil sharpener with a picture of a rabbit on it. You know, Grandma, because of him I was able to finish writing my page of 'Long Live Mao!' Professor Yang said that I traced the characters well, but that I can still do better."

Rubbing her forehead, my grandmother interrupted me, "Excuse me, Niu-Niu, but since I paid for school, I thought they furnished pencil sharpeners."

She reached under the bed to take out the paper in which our savings were hidden and held out two five-fen coins to buy a pencil sharpener. There were so few coins there, the largest being only five maos, that I gave it back on the pretext that Chou Chiang would be pleased to lend me his. But she insisted. "Don't worry, my darling, even if I have to bleed my-self white, I'll do my best so you have what you need to study. Now that the propaganda posters are everywhere, there's much more paper to salvage. And I could do the trash cans in the evenings . . ." No matter what she said, I had decided to put back the ten fens secretly that very evening.

I noticed suddenly that she had not touched her plate which was only half-filled, thinking no doubt that my stories would take the place of a meal. I urged her to eat and remembered to give Professor Yang's respects. Carrying the bowl to her mouth with one hand, she dried her tears of joy with the other, stammering, "Niu-Niu, you don't know how happy your par-ents and your grandfather would be if they saw you today."

In the evening before going to bed, I opened my notebook already covered with "Long Live Mao," and put it on the table near the window. Why didn't people like Grandpa who lived on the moon ever return? Why did my parents have to work on the other side of the world? Why did Grandma, Professor

Yang and Chou Chiang show me so much affection? I had the incredible chance to go to school like a normal child and I was convinced that our life would get better from now on. I opened my eyes wide to look through the window, where my grandfather was supposed to appear to answer my questions, to correct my writing . . . but he didn't show up, not even in my dreams.

Chapter 9
DISORIENTED

The school was on a small street not far from our house. According to my grandmother, it had originally been an old temple filled with smoke from burning incense; the faithful sometimes came from a great distance. The chanting of the monks, punctuated by the rattle of prayer wheels, echoed in one's head even after one left the temple.

Of course, the revolutionaries had pillaged it as they had all the other temples. But Mao's order, *Go forth and multiply*, had been so well obeyed that the schools were overcrowded. The temple, therefore, had been reclaimed. The setting was magnificent, of course. The inner garden was used for gymnastics. Of the four large rooms, one was reserved for the teachers, while the others were classrooms. There were only a few tables for our use. The blackboard was simply a painted square on the wall. There were no chairs, no notebooks, no books, although Mao's Little Red Book was in plentiful supply. Nothing, however, could dampen my eagerness which was rewarded each day with something new.

Professor Yang taught us a new song: "The East is red, the sun rises, China brought forth a Mao Zedung. He devotes himself to his people, he is the great star of our redemption."

On Saturday in front of an effigy of Mao, the gym teacher had us practice the steps of a dance symbolizing "loyalty." The art teacher taught us how to paint a large red sun with gigantic golden rays under which we learned to write, "Long Live Mao."

I had no trouble with singing and dancing but drawing class was more complicated. The sun had to be perfectly round and crayons were always necessary. Chou Chiang's drawing was radiant with bright red, next to mine that was a sad grey, because all I had was a regular pencil. I was so ashamed. I would have sacrificed three days' food for a packet of color crayons. I saw again our miserable savings in their envelope and I knew that there wasn't enough to pay for that.

In the afternoon, after the revolutionary song had been sung and all the students were standing in line in the courtyard ready to leave for the day, Professor Yang called my name in front of everyone. I didn't know what I had done and looked around in a panic, while the others quietly left. I was petrified when she approached me. She took me gently by the hand and asked me why I had not handed in my sun. How did she know? I thought naively that the art teacher had told on me. When I showed it to Professor Yang, she turned pale and asked, "Why is it black?" I looked down at my shoes and told her why. Professor Yang made sure that no one was watching and promptly tore up my drawing, cramming the pieces into her pocket. Without a word, she led me into the street, as if she were afraid of something. We came to a little store where she pointed to a packet of crayons, made sure that there was a red one there, then offered it to me. "Here, Niu-Niu, never color the sun black again."

My head down, my lips closed, I didn't dare to take the packet because I felt so guilty at having caused her a problem. She forced the crayons into my hand, saying with a smile, "You draw well . . . . It only lacks a bit of red. Please do the drawing again for tomorrow." I bowed very low, but she stopped me. "Niu-Niu, if you run into difficulties again, don't bother your grandmother. Just come talk to me."

"Why are you so kind to me? You don't hate me because I'm a child of criminals?"

"You're a sweet little girl. Don't ever tell me again that you're the child of criminals. If your grandmother heard that, she'd be very unhappy. I'm your teacher and I care about you. If you want me to go on being nice to you, you must be a serious student and get the best grades. I'm sure that soon your grandmother and I will be very proud of you." I swore before Heaven that I would not let them down. After a tender goodbye we separated.

I walked along with my eyes riveted on my packet of crayons as if it were a compass. It was so beautifully decorated, I was overcome. To me, it was more than a present, it was proof of Professor Yang's affection. My heart was bursting with gratitude.

Confidently I told Chou Chiang the story of the drawing.

"Oh, all black!" he said.

"What's so strange about that? You look as scared as a mouse!"

His raised eyebrows looked like the roof of a pagoda, and his mouth made a full moon. That made me laugh. Pompous as a grown-up, he lectured me. "Don't you know that the sun must absolutely be red? It's a terrible mistake to make it dark. Especially never black . . . . Here, I've got a little roll for you."

"Why do you always bring me rolls? Aren't you hungry?"

"We have lots at my house! My father even has a car. Does your father have a car too?"

How could he have a car? Hardly anybody had one. In any case, I couldn't even remember my father's face. I was afraid

Chou Chiang was going to ask me some other embarrassing question. "It's time to go. Grandma will worry."

At home I sat on the wooden doorstep, waiting for my grandmother to return and I let my thoughts wander. Why *was* the sun red? Why did this frighten Professor Yang and Chou Chiang? What does the word "revolutionary" really mean? Was Mao an emperor or a god? Why was he worshiped while everyone hated us?

Of course, I bore a grudge against the Cultural Revolution. To me it meant the self-criticism sessions, the beatings, the insults, the hunger, the cold, the disappearance of my parents, the murder of my grandfather and my grandmother's tears. Yet so many people seemed to participate in this great movement with so much enthusiasm! Everywhere there were propaganda posters in the streets, clouds of red flags, slogans all over, hymns to the glory of that greatest of wise men, Mao, who had miraculously found a way of making himself beloved. Should I go to see Mao, whose followers had caused me so much unhappiness? When I asked Grandma about it, she wiped her eyes and told me to just be a good little girl.

At school I studied eagerly to get the best grades so as not to disappoint Professor Yang. When it was my turn to clean the classroom, I polished the tables and windows until they shone. Each time I imagined that Mao, whose portrait lighted up the room, was looking at me and that one day, thanks to my diligence, he would consider lifting his punishment, no longer treating my parents as criminals. It was my way of helping them.

During dance class on Saturday, in front of the precious effigy, I gave my all until I was covered with sweat. The slightest misstep plunged me into gloom. At the end of one session, Chou Chiang whispered to me, "You're pretty when you dance!"

His compliment left me speechless, overcome with pleasure. I made a vow to return his friendship a hundredfold. So I did his chores for him, swept the classroom in his place. I also offered him a beautiful stone that my grandfather had found when he was working and that I had jealously guarded until then. As for him, he was twice as nice, giving me rolls to eat and more pencils. Besides this, he shared a secret with me: he told me about an underground passageway in our neighborhood that led to an abandoned theater.

One day he secretly took me there and after that we often went there together, to turn somersaults on the stage and yell at the top of our lungs and have a great time. We pretended to put on a play: while one of us was playing the clown on the stage, the other was wildly applauding in the auditorium. We used the curtains to climb on or to play hide-and-seek. We had discovered transparent colored papers on the projectors, which we could turn on and bathe our world in red, blue or green. This was our special place and we shared it with no one.

One afternoon after class, Chou Chiang invited me to play at his house. When we entered the inner garden, a vague memory stirred in me. This house resembled our former home and once again I suddenly remembered how my parents were taken away. There was a spacious living room with a large couch, a delicately decorated table on one of the beautiful rugs that covered the floor and pretty paintings on the wall. I recognized a reproduction of *The Woman with the Peony* by T'ang Ying; my grandmother had shown me a photo of it. Chou Chiang's father had to be rich.

Chou Chiang's room was overflowing with toys: a small train, little plastic figures, comic books in abundance — a whole marvelous universe that whirled before my eyes like a kaleidoscope. While we were playing with a wooden construction toy, I saw a photo of Chou Chiang with his father. The man looked familiar, but before I could remember where I had seen him, Chou Chiang's mother entered the room and looked me over from head to toe. I became self-conscious about my dirty patched clothes, my toes showing through my torn shoes.

"Mama, this is Niu-Niu, my classmate."

"What a strange name!"

Paralyzed with fright, I greeted her with a bow, but she ignored me, saying to her son, "Dear, you have to change your clothes to see Aunt Zhang."

He didn't obey right away, saying that he would like to play with me a little longer. Irritated, his mother looked at me.

"Where do you live? What do your parents do?"

I answered that they worked far away and that I lived alone with my grandmother.

"Where is your grandfather?"

This was decidedly not the place for me. I preferred to get my things together and leave.

"Her grandfather is dead."

"Ah so, what did he die of?"

I had told Chou Chiang that my grandfather had died following an illness. I didn't want to tell that lie again, a lie I had told reluctantly. I was turning toward the door when Chou Chiang's mother slapped her forehead angrily. "Oh, I remember who you are! Yes, of course, your name is Niu-Niu and your grandfather was Liu T'ai-Lung, the criminal who committed suicide. That's it!"

My arms and legs felt as if they had been jolted by an electrical shock, my face was getting red and I was hot as if the fire inside me was about to explode. She was lying. My grandfather did not commit suicide. He died from a beating, from the Red Guards' rifle butts. The image of Chou Chiang's father came back clearly to my mind. Suddenly I remembered where I had seen him before. He was the head of the Red Guards who had given the order to finish off my grandfather. Before I could open my mouth to answer Madame Chou's accusations, she tore into me with insults. "Really, you have no shame! To dare play with my son! To dare come here! But just look at yourself, you're all in rags! Your stink contaminates the house. Get out of here!"

She took hold of my schoolbag and threw it across the threshold. I was shocked and so ashamed I could have died. My tears dissolved my courage, preventing me from lashing back at this awful creature.

I picked up my bag and left that terrible place, paying no attention to Chou Chiang's entreaties. I hated him and his parents and I hated my whole family who had inflicted this terrible punishment on me. Everywhere I was considered the black cat that brought bad luck. Always. When I got home, I threw myself weeping on the bed. Nonplused, my grandmother wanted to know if I had misbehaved at school. Her question only increased my feeling of injustice. There was no one I could confide in about my shame and my anger.

"Everywhere I go I have problems! Everyone seems to think I'm a bird of bad omen. Everyone runs away from me. Even Chou Chiang won't talk to me any more! Now are you satisfied? It was *his father* who killed Grandpa! His mother called me all kinds of names and chased me out of their house! How horrible the world is! I detest you! Why are you criminals? What did you do? Why do you have to be my family?"

For the first time ever, my grandmother slapped me really hard across the face. I didn't weep, I didn't cry out — I was that dumbfounded. Grandma pitched into me like the others. She called me an idiot and told me not to waste my tears on the son of my grandfather's murderer. "How could you forget that man's barbarity! He's a Red Guard — they took your parents away and you play with their children! How can you hate your parents so much?"

"But Chou Chiang is my only friend. No one else speaks a word to me."

"Even if everyone shuns you, you're not to play with him!"

"I'm going to! I'll go to his house and play with him! If you're going to hit me, where can I turn? Everyone treats me like dirt!"

My grandmother suddenly seemed to become faint — these attacks had come over her ever since my grandfather's death. I hurried to her side. "Grandma, what's the matter? You're not well! Forgive me, Grandma. Don't get angry! Everything will be fine."

Slowly she staggered to the bed and collapsed. Her heart was beating much too fast and her skin was like ice.

"Grandma, are you all right? Would you like some water? Tell me where it hurts."

Overcome with panic, I wept in helpless fear. She waved her hand to tell me that she only wanted a little bit of rest. I stayed next to her, watching her. She breathed deeply, as tears seeped from under her closed eyes.

What did it all mean? Were we so evil? Was it impossible for the others to accept an old lady and a little girl? Were we worth less than a pig or a dog?

She opened her eyes. "Forgive me, Niu-Niu, for having slapped you," she said gently. "I swore when your parents left that I would never hurt you . . . ."

I stammered, "No, it's me, it's my fault!"

We were both shaken. She told me to accept things and not to ask myself any more questions.

That evening I made dinner. While we were eating, Grandma kept saying what good people my parents were and how they were incapable of doing anything bad, that they deserved my love and respect. I believed her. But after dinner, when I was quietly hunched over the matchboxes, behind my calm demeanor I was filled with anxiety and confusion at the ways of the world.

When I saw Chou Chiang again, I didn't say a word to him, I didn't even look at him. I couldn't stop thinking that his father had beaten my grandfather to death and his mother had chased me out of his house. He no longer tried to talk to me either. But when I needed a pencil sharpener, he silently handed me his. Even though he didn't say anything, I felt more than ever how goodhearted he was.

After class, we walked separately, a few steps apart along the street, keeping the same heavy silence. If he got too far ahead of me, he slowed down. If I got ahead, I stopped to tie my shoelaces. If I hadn't promised my grandmother, I would have broken the silence. This went on until one day Professor Yang called me to her office.

"Niu-Niu, have you quarreled with Chou Chiang?"

I didn't know what to say.

"You were always inseparable. Why this distance now? Did he hurt you or say something bad? Tell me what happened."

I hesitated. "Professor Yang, is it true that you don't hate me?"

"Of course not, Niu-Niu."

"Then why does everyone else hate me? Chou Chiang's mother won't let him play with me, and my grandmother too . . ."

She understood. Touching me on the shoulder to calm me, she thought a moment before asking, "Niu-Niu, do you want to be friends again with Chou Chiang?"

Without hesitation, I nodded "yes." Professor Yang went to talk to him.

A few days later, Chou Chiang came to find me and said, "Let's be best friends in the world again. Okay?"

"You want to?"

He smiled in answer. I was filled with happiness. His smile swept away all my anxieties and put my chaotic world back in order. We were both so happy at our reunion that we didn't want to lose that afternoon. Together we sneaked into the public park without paying, to steal wild fruit and gather small pebbles by the brook.

If his parents had not been who they were, if his father had not killed my grandfather, our happiness would have been unblemished. If I hadn't been traumatized by the hateful scorn to which I was subjected because of my family, our childish pleasure would have been perfect. If we could have been joined forever as we were that afternoon, if life could have taken a step backward, my heart would have been filled with ineffable bliss. In spite of everything, I wasn't too far from this happiness, but everything within me doubted whether I was really entitled to it.

Chapter 10
THE OUTLAW GANG

Chou Chiang and I had to be secretive about playing together. He apologized for this and tried to make me feel better by blaming his mother, but he didn't need to. My faith in him had been restored; as my only real friend, he was precious to me. I appreciated him as I wished others would appreciate me.

Whether or not my grandmother was aware of our reconciliation, she never let on. Her good heart and her sensitivity told her that children should not carry on their parents' hatreds. Nevertheless, Chou Chiang and I were careful not to flaunt our friendship.

In his absence, I had found out that I rather enjoyed solitude. Dawdling on the stoop of our hovel, I watched the dying leaves fall, birds on the wing or a magnificent sunset. After I tired of these diversions, I had time to take care of Mei Lin's cat before returning to the tedium of my lonely cage.

A rumor began to circulate in town which soon aroused my curiosity. I overheard a conversation in the street that some young gun-toting bandits on horseback, with girls riding behind them, came out under cover of night to rob, kill and burn. I loved these scary stories. Everyone told them — even the shyest among us had his own version: "My older brother ran across them at dusk. There were about a dozen of them and this pretty girl was with them too. They had guns and one of them had a large sack. My brother was really scared, but they acted kind and they even asked him to join them. When he said he couldn't because he had to take care of his poor family, the leader gave him some money, and said, 'We only kill the rich, but we help the poor. If you're having troubles, come see us. We'll help you.'"

We remained skeptical, but the older brother confirmed the story. Feeling important, he said he would help us if we wanted to contact the gang. From that time on, our shy friend basked in the limelight.

When night fell, terrified adults doublelocked their doors, but children found excitement in the danger and mystery.

Another schoolmate also had an experience with these bandits: he was coming back from the country with his mother when some soldiers ran right past them to surround a building. "Some people around us yelled, 'The killers are in that building!' We were panicked; we hid in a doorway and saw everything. Suddenly there was gunfire and we heard bullets hitting near us. In the wink of an eye, the soldiers ran away; they left their wounded and some of their weapons behind. Then the bandits came out of the building, revolvers in each hand. They were young, but they certainly knew how to shoot."

"And the soldiers didn't chase them?"

"No, the soldiers took off like the wind. The bandits are invincible. They say that before they enter a town, they let the police know. But they've never been arrested."

"Do they look like demons?"

"No, they're like us, with two feet and two hands."

After we heard that, our imaginations went wild. We were distracted even during class to the point where our teachers had to call a general assembly to warn us. They also asked parents to stop talking about the outlaws in front of us. But the excitement only increased.

While going through the garbage cans, Grandmother had made the acquaintance of Grandmother Lei. This poor woman was old and illiterate and very kindhearted; she often visited with my grandma. I heard her talking about how before the "Liberation," she had sold hot tea on the streets and shared a simple, but happy life with her husband, a rickshaw driver. After the "Liberation," and up to the end of the "Great Leap Forward," their life improved somewhat. Then the storm hit them. Her husband was killed by a stray bullet. She was left with a son who gave her two grandchildren, a girl and a boy, for whom she now lived. When the Cultural Revolution began, her son was condemned to nine years in a reeducation camp without her ever knowing why. Every day Party officials would come, trying to convince her daughter-in-law to divorce the son in order "to remain on the straight and narrow" or risk her husband's fate. The young woman would at first have preferred death to such dishonor. Her colleagues at work, however, would no longer speak to her. She was demoted, her salary cut in half. People spat on her.

At the end of her rope, the daughter-in-law signed the divorce papers. This forced her to move out with her daughter, but, with a heavy heart, she left her son behind. From then on the daughter-in-law did not dare visit the family for fear of violating the Party line.

"There is no morality left in China," said Grandmother Lei. "We still lived close to each other. I often saw her watching her son from a distance." This same son, when he reached the age of twenty, got hold of a rifle and killed two policemen to avenge his father. "The police are looking for him everywhere. I've had no news of him for a year now. I weep night and day . . . ."

One evening, Grandmother Lei came to talk to Grandma. When she said she thought her grandson was a member of what the neighborhood called the "gang of killers," Grandma couldn't agree with her. "All your grandson did was avenge his father, but this is a dangerous, destructive gang!"

"Oh, you think so, Mrs Liu?"

Suddenly, the old woman jumped up and carefully closed our door and window. The she sat down again next to Grandma. From her bodice, she took out a crumpled piece of paper. "This was pushed under my door last night. Could you read it to me?"

Grandma read out the note in the candlelight. "My dear Grandmother, it's me, your little dragon. I miss you very much. How are you? Please don't worry about me. I'm doing fine. Take care of your health, don't cry too much and you'll make me happy. I'll try to see you soon. Your beloved grandson."

Grandmother Lei, who listened as though she were hypnotized, burst into tears. "The Lord be praised, he's still alive! He was so good to me and so devoted to his father. Poor boy! I never dreamt that at my age my family would be destroyed and I would be all alone. We need each other so much."

"Don't worry! I'm sure your son is also alive! For your little dragon's sake, you should take care of yourself."

"You're right! For his sake, I'm going to eat well, sleep well and calm my soul."

Just as she was leaving, she turned and said, "You know, Mrs Liu, many people say this gang is not so bad. They only attack the rich and not the little people. Have they ever hurt anyone on our street?"

It was afternoon and I had finished my homework before going out into the street with the cat. There I found innumerable posters showing the picture of a young man, identified only as a dangerous criminal. I assumed that this meant that there would soon be an execution, which was always preceded by the criminal being paraded through town in the back of a truck. However, no date was given.

Then I took the underground passage to the old theater, hoping to unearth some new treasure. Chou Chiang had told me that some years earlier, when a Russian attack was feared, many such shelters for artists had been built. Once the danger had passed, these were forgotten. It smelled of mildew down there and the floor was strewn with trash. Here and there strange molds were growing in the darkness. It was so spooky I regretted having ventured there alone. At the far end of the stage, I noticed an open door that we had never been able to force. My heart pounding, I slipped through, went down a corridor and entered one of the rooms. I stopped in my tracks, my eyes wide. In the half-closed drawers of a pretty, rose-colored vanity, I could see ribbons, make-up accessories, all kinds of wonderful things. Feverishly I began to stuff my pockets, but to do this, I had to put down the cat, which promptly ran off. I began looking for him in every corner of this sinister place, but I couldn't find him. Overcome by fear and cold, I was just about ready to quit and come back the next day, when I saw a form move in the darkness before me. I thought I saw eyes glowing and the shape of a nose. A ghost! I screamed in terror, but the phantom put its hand over my mouth. I was covered with cold sweat and felt weak. Ready to faint, I was going to attempt one last shout for help when the thing whispered to me, "Don't be afraid. I'm not a ghost," but that's what they all say before they eat you.

"If you stop screaming, I'll let you go."

I was going to take advantage of this and run for it, but when he released me, all I could do was to shake without saying a word. I could feel his breath on my paralyzed neck. I closed my eyes tightly so I wouldn't see him when he ate me, but nothing happened. I turned around with a start. What was this? It was a tall young man, completely normal, and with the loveliest smile to boot.

"So it's true you're not a demon. You're not going to eat me up, are you?"

Even though he nodded reassuringly, I continued to eye him with suspicion. He asked me to touch his hands. "You see, they're warm. Ghosts' hands are always cold." It was true. I relaxed and smiled at him, but a sound from the outside made him wary. Then nothing more.

"Go see if someone is in the theater, but don't tell them I'm here." I remained paralyzed. "Go quickly, or I'll eat you!" but I was already on my way out.

There was no one in the theater and I would gladly have left if I had found my cat. I told him there was no one there. He seemed relieved and asked me my name. I spoke as little as possible, feeling uneasy.

"You're brave, Niu-Niu," he flattered me. Of course, that was enough for me, so I dared ask him what he was doing here.

"Everyone is after me to kill me out there."

"Why? Is it the outlaw gang who are after you because you're rich?"

He looked at me, very surprised. "How come you know about the gang?"

"That's all they talk about at school."

"If you met one of the gang, would you be afraid?"

"Not at all. It seems they don't kill the poor, and me, I'm very poor!"

"You're funny!"

"You too!" He was decidedly likeable. In a short while, we became friendly. I asked him who he was.

"I'm a member of the gang. Right now the police are looking for me everywhere. I can't leave, but don't be afraid, Niu-Niu . . ."

It didn't occur to me! This was an unheard-of chance, this opportunity to meet someone like him. I could show off at school! A thousand questions suddenly popped into my mind. "Why are you a member? Who are the others? Why have you killed so many people?" I asked them all in one breath.

Gently, he put his arm around me and told me his story. He said that they were not criminals. All his companions had been high-school students living with their families. At the beginning of the Cultural Revolution, their teachers had encouraged them to criticize those who were called subversives. All of them had been delighted to take part in the movement. They organized huge meetings to criticize criminals. They hoisted red flags, waved Mao's Little Red Book and took trains to demonstrate in other cities throughout China. They even went all the way to Beijing. "And there we saw Mao on top of Tiananmen Square."

"How was he?"

"He was ugly!"

"But no, I've seen his picture everywhere. He's beautiful! You don't love him?"

"No, he's an old swindler!"

I was shocked. How dared he talk that way about our own great star?

"We had all worshipped Mao Zedung and sacrificed everything for him, because he said we had to clear out old ideas to build a new society, a new China. That was exactly what we wanted to do. After we came back from Beijing, we went on believing in those slogans. But everything turned upside down. Mao's men told us that everything we did was wrong, that we had to mend our ways. We couldn't make head or tail of that, so we continued our movement. We were completely disoriented. Naturally, such parallel actions were dangerous to Mao. He considered himself an emperor, while we wanted a new China."

"But my grandmother told me he was already an emperor, even though in China you can't call him that. I know someone who named his son, 'Mao Zedung' and he died for it!"

He became silent. After a heavy sigh, he continued, "Then the army, soldiers with rifles, came to gun us down. Many of the young were killed. The others, if they didn't end up in prison, fled to the mountains, but even there the army chased them down. We had no choice: to continue staying alive, we had to turn the guns on them. We've never killed the people, just party officials. Gradually other young men joined us . . . all the outcasts."

"I heard that you each had two revolvers. Is that true?"

"And what's more, we're good shots. Here, look . . ." He showed me a big handgun: it felt cold and was heavy to lift, but it wasn't that impressive.

"How did the police find out that you're hiding in this area?"

"When I went to see my grandmother, I was recognized. A few years ago, when the army was after us, I came back home because we didn't dare continue the fight. One day my grandmother told me that my father had been sent to prison because some official that he had quarreled with had lodged a false accusation against him. This official was like some vulture. Later I learned my best friend was murdered by soldiers. I became so angry that I stole a gun and killed the man who put my father behind bars and I killed a cop at the same time. They searched for me everywhere. That's why I joined the gang."

"And where's your grandma now?"

He lowered his eyes and told me the street where his grandmother lived. It was really a small world, for it was Grandmother Lei!

"Do you really know her, Niu-Niu? Tell me quickly, is she well?"

"Yes, she and my grandmother are good friends. Every day they go to salvage paper from the trash cans."

"The poor thing! She's so old and still has to rummage in garbage cans to make a living! All this because of these bastards who have taken it out on our family. I'll kill them all!"

"Are there any children in your gang? I'd like to join too, to avenge my family."

He felt sorry for me and hugged me, promising to talk to the leader and I promised to tell his grandmother I had seen him. Like children we grasped each other's little finger, swearing, "One, two, three, he who doesn't keep his promise will be split in two by lightning."

He then asked me to find him some food, since he had been hiding for two days with nothing to eat. Apparently he didn't know about the secret passage, so I proudly showed it to him.

With my teeth chattering, I walked along the street, feeling that everyone saw what I was doing. I started to run, faster and faster, and in passing the posters, I realized that the picture of the criminal was that of my new friend hidden in the theater. I prayed hard that he would make it safe and sound.

Terribly excited, I told my grandma everything. She looked a little worried, but finally smiled affectionately at me. "Niu-Niu, you're really brave. You did the right thing, but don't breathe a word to anyone or Grandmother Lei will have lots of trouble."

From that time on, we lived anxiously awaiting bad news about the gang. Two months later we heard the army had surrounded the house where they were hiding. They spent a whole day negotiating, but finally, it was said, the young men all committed suicide. Not one was taken. Others claimed that the army had fired at them for hours, that it had been a carnage, that several had tried to escape, but had been caught by the soldiers. For those it was prison for life, and that included the girl who was with them. With all the different versions of the story, one thing was clear: the outlaw gang was gone.

The town regained its calm. No one spoke of the gang of outlaws any more. It was finally over. These poor champions of justice had vanished, ground up in the pitiless cogwheels of a society gone mad.

Chapter 11

THE CHILDREN'S
REBELLION

After the disappearance of the outlaw gang, the whole world seemed grey. A story had ended and life in school reverted to what it always had been. We no longer talked about it.

Summer came again and added a new year to make me seven years old. I had grown physically and my mind had matured. I knew more things: that Mao deserved a long life and criminals deserved death. The sun had to be colored red and we had to pursue the Revolution to the end.

My circle comprised Chou Chiang, Professor Yang and a few others. There were some things you couldn't question: that was just the way things were. This way of thinking helped me to accept and deal with the world.

Summer brought flowers and heat, as well as some new developments at school. At the end of the first school year, the professors were planning to choose the best students in three disciplines: intellectual studies, manual skills and singing. First, each of the three classes had to elect its four best students.

To qualify, I cleaned the room and the windows especially well, and studied more than usual in order to get the best grade in each subject. I was encouraged by Mao's portrait. No sacrifice seemed too great to thwart the series of misfortunes that had struck my family. I finally received enough votes from the students to reward me for my patience and determination. The four pupils chosen had to wait for the professors' final decision. Whoever made it to the end was privileged to receive the famous red scarf directly from the hands of the teachers, while the audience applauded. It was a tremendous honor for the pupil who was considered a model of conduct for his or her schoolmates.

Professor Yang told us that the red scarf represented the red flag, the color of which stood for the blood of the Liberation's martyrs. It was the symbol of the country. Children my age had grown up under the red flag, thanks to a Party that guaranteed us a life as sweet as honey. It was only proper, therefore, that we express our heartfelt gratitude with a fervor as bright as the flag itself, that we love our country and Mao Zedung, that we live and die for them. It behooved us to follow in the footsteps of these martyrs and to continue the Revolution.

I was convinced, as each pupil was, that all of this was of vital importance. I was eager to be elected so that my heart would be bright red and that Grandma would be proud of me. I was finally chosen among the four candidates and needed only the teachers' approval. With this sword of Damocles hanging over my head, I closely watched their faces. One week passed and all the children were as nervous as ants on a hot stove.

Professor Yang came to find me. "Niu-Niu, you're a lovely little girl, very intelligent and conscientious . . . ."

Shyly I protested, but I was flattered. I was convinced that Professor Yang was going to tell me that she was proud of my having been chosen. I beamed at her. But she seemed sad. She took me by the hand, and gave a deep sigh.

"Professor Yang, I was chosen, wasn't I?" I was so impatient to hear her say "yes."

With tears in her eyes, she smiled at me. "Niu-Niu, you like me a lot, don't you? If you want to, I'll take you to the park after school."

"Oh, thank you. I'll go tell Chou Chiang."

After class we went to her place first. She shared a room with the art teacher, who was there when we came in: it had a cooking stove, a bookshelf, two single beds, and two dressers. It was so clean. She offered each of us two candies, and said, "Niu-Niu, I have a beautiful present for you. Guess what it is!"

"A pencil?"

"No."

"A pencil sharpener?"

She smiled mysteriously and took a flowered dress from a suitcase under her bed. I was in seventh heaven and threw myself into her arms. I was also feeling good that I had deserved to be chosen.

"It's nothing, Niu-Niu. You're a big girl now. I like to see you looking pretty."

Chou Chiang turned his back and I quickly tried on the dress, while Professor Yang clapped with pleasure. But the art teacher was looking at me strangely. She didn't seem friendly. She whispered something to Professor Yang, who furiously took her by the arm.

"How dare you! She's only a child." I supposed it had something to do with me, but I was so happy over Professor Yang's beautiful gift, I didn't pay much attention. Holding hands, we left for the park.

We ran first to the swings, then to the slide. After Professor Yang took us on a rowboat around the lake, she asked me to sit on the grass so she could take my picture. I've kept that photo to this day.

She went back to our house with me. I was ashamed of it

because it was so dirty and messy. My grandmother tried to pick things up, but she couldn't really hide the condition of our hovel.

Professor Yang tried to reassure her. "Don't worry, Grandmother. A glass of water would be nice. I can't stay long. I have to talk to you . . ."

She seemed uncomfortable with me in the room, so Grandmother sent me to fetch a pail of water to boil for tea.

The place where we got our water was quite far from the house. I guessed that something was being hidden from me. When I returned, Professor Yang had already left.

In the evening after dinner, Grandma asked me to sit beside her, so she could talk to me about something serious. "Niu-Niu, Professor Yang and I know that you are a serious girl . . . I have to tell you . . . But you mustn't be sad . . ."

What was happening now? Grandma's voice was disquieting. I was afraid I had done something stupid.

"Professor Yang told me that you weren't . . . that you weren't chosen as the best in your class . . . but that's not serious, because the other students elected you just the same. Professor Yang doesn't want you to be sad. Perhaps the next time . . ."

"But why? I was elected, I could even be picked as the best in the whole school! Grandma, what do the teachers have against me?"

"Nothing . . . It's just that . . . You're not quite good enough. There are others who are better than you. I love you, Niu-Niu and so does Professor Yang. Try the next time . . . the next time . . ."

I didn't want to cry. I bit my lips in order to bear the blow, but this was too difficult. My heart had turned to ice and told me that there would be no next time.

The following day I found a bit of cloth in the trash can and

I put it around my neck. There, I had just awarded myself the honorary scarf; it wasn't red, but it was even prettier and it helped me to bear the award ceremony. Chou Chiang won the prize for intellectual studies.

Shortly afterwards, the whole school stopped classes to go to the countryside to help the farmers weed their fields and put on natural fertilizer. The teachers had explained to us that this was part of a scholastic program called "Studying in the Country." In the future we would have other educational programs in the factory and in the army. These activities were essential to raise the level of the country and to stop Revisionism. For us, it was an occasion to play outdoors. We played catch, ran around, looked for wild fruit. As for Revisionism, we didn't even know what that was.

During the two weeks of our rural stay, Professor Yang often seemed deep in her own thoughts, as if she had lost her joy in life. She kept apart. Chou Chiang and I went to talk to her.

"Professor Yang, aren't you feeling well? Are you tired?"

She remained quiet and we followed her up to the little river and gazed at the sunset together.

"Professor Yang, we have many medicines at our house if you need anything . . . ." But she kept her silence, which was broken only by the sound of the splashing waters.

"You're my favorite students, but I don't know if I bring you luck." She continued talking, as though to herself. "They say it's a world without love . . . . It's really complicated to want to do good for one's fellow man."

"What's wrong, Professor Yang?"

"Niu-Niu, Chou Chiang, when you're grown up, you must be goodhearted people, even if it takes great effort and courage. You must be kind."

The sun was already setting on the horizon and the breeze carried the sound of the gong which called the farmers home. The cawing of the crows sounded ominous, like a funeral dirge.

At the end of our stay in the country, the peasants invited us to a "celebration of bitter memories and sweet thoughts." In the tiny village square, all the schoolchildren sat on the ground to listen to the people tell their stories. They told us that before the Liberation, the landowners had treated them badly, beaten them, deprived them of food. A year of their labor was not enough to pay their taxes; they had to sell their children in order to survive. After the Liberation, they had enough to eat and comfortable houses. Their dead children had been consecrated as martyrs to the Revolution. Our hosts urged us never to forget the harshness of life before, so that we would appreciate how it was nowadays. They served us a meal fitting the occasion to close the ceremony — a dish of "bitter memories and sweet thoughts" made of a mixture of corn and vegetables. I found nothing bitter in it and filled myself up without asking any questions.

An old peasant woman repeated that life was much better, that everything was going well now, rambling on and on, eager to repeat her lesson. Professor Yang laughed gently at her under the stern eye of the art teacher.

This interlude over, we prepared to go back to our everyday existence.

Two weeks later, Professor Yang was teaching us as usual when suddenly some men entered the room and stopped the class, shouting insults at her. "For a long time you've been hiding your opposition to the Revolution, but paper cannot hide a fire. The guilty are always discovered!"

They tied her hands behind her back and took her away. She did not resist and allowed herself to be arrested without a word. We were all in a state of shock, calling out to Professor Yang with heart-rending cries.

The leader of the Red Guard detachment was of course Chou Chiang's father, who pounded on the desk to make us stop. "Students! She is no longer your teacher. She's been a counterrevolutionary for a long time. She has committed many evil acts that you couldn't understand. She even dared to speak ill of the great Mao. All the children of this school must despise and hate her. Each of you must write an essay denouncing her."

He departed, leaving us dumbfounded. How could Professor Yang be against the Revolution? It was another one of their lies. She was nice to all the children and taught us unfailingly to *Love Mao, love the Party*. Never had we heard her utter a word against Mao!

The class fell silent, trying to understand what had happened. No one moved. Suddenly I became very angry. I felt like exploding. I looked Chou Chiang squarely in the eye, "That's another trick of your father's. Why is he so nasty?"

The others overheard and turned to look at the poor boy who lowered his eyes, wet with tears. Instantly I regretted my words. Chou Chiang loved Professor Yang as much as I did.

No one left the room at noon. The only sounds were those of students eating. Outside in the courtyard the professors were whispering and pacing nervously up and down.

At the beginning of the afternoon, the art teacher finally arrived, announcing in a dry voice, "Your Professor of Chinese is no longer the principal of this school. She is a bad element in society. She's always been in touch with criminals.

She's gone so far as to allow their children to be enrolled in our school. This is unacceptable. As of today, I will be your main teacher. Our first task is to cleanse your minds, which have been polluted by Professor Yang."

Chou Chiang rose from his seat to shout at her, "It's you, you're the poisoner, the evil one! I know it. It's you who said bad things about Professor Yang."

The class erupted into chaos. The rebellious Chou Chiang went on. "I swear this on my life!"

All the pupils rose from their seats, shaking their fists at the art teacher. "We want Professor Yang! We don't want you! Get out! Leave!"

Red with confusion, she did not know what to do. "Chou Chiang, I will inform your father of your foolishness."

But her voice was drowned out by our yelling. There was nothing for her to do but leave the room. We all gathered around Chou Chiang to congratulate him. "Great! You're really brave. Tell us, Chou Chiang, aren't you scared of your father?"

Very moved, he assured us that he was not afraid. He seemed to have taken it upon himself to save Professor Yang. One student asked if it was true that the art teacher had denounced our dear professor.

"Yes, these last few days the art teacher's been coming to our house all the time and I listened at the door. She told my father that Professor Yang was a bad person. The art teacher said she found 'subversive comments' in her diary. Then she said that Professor Yang was not a good principal for the school and that *she* could run it better. But I didn't believe all her lies. She's jealous!"

Our hair stood on end and we all began to call her names. The math teacher came in to scold us — we had acted badly toward the art teacher and if we continued, the other teachers would call for a meeting with the parents.

Classes were canceled for the afternoon and we were told to go home to prepare ourselves for a meeting to criticize Professor Yang that would take place the following Saturday. All the pupils would have to speak up.

At the corner of the street we all swore not to be afraid of our parents or of the consequences of what we were about to do — above all, to avoid saying anything bad about our beloved teacher. The one who broke the oath would be an outcast.

The day arrived. The size of the crowd and the imposing presence of the parents threw some cold water on our determination. And then there was Professor Yang. She was in the same position as my grandparents had been, hands tied behind her back and a sign around her neck with the words "Counterrevolutionary." They had shaved half her head to shame her, to show that she was now but half a person, one of the dregs of humanity. She seemed to have aged several years.

Chou Chiang's father announced that the art teacher would run the school and that we should be polite and obedient under the threat of expulsion.

Each of the teachers read his or her denunciation. The longest talk was, of course, that of the hateful new headmistress. As we had agreed, we listened silently with our heads bowed. The teachers began to worry, but it was too late. "Students, say something!"

But we remained silent. A quiet chuckle spread through our rows — that was good for these mean teachers! The traitor came down to the podium and approached us to talk to the head of our class. "Didn't you write an essay of denunciation? Then go to the podium and read it."

Without leaving time for reflection, she pulled him by the sleeve. He was shaking all over under our harsh gaze. He had no right to say anything against Professor Yang, who had been very nice to him.

He unfolded a piece of paper, looked at our professor, looked around at the other teachers and the Red Guards seated at the end of the platform. Suddenly he showed a kind of bravery that surprised us all by loudly declaring, "I don't know this text. I can't read it! I didn't write it, I don't understand the characters."

What a genius! We all began to clap and our dear Professor Yang raised her head, tears in her eyes, to smile at us. We knew that smile well, but today it seemed so pathetic that it tied our stomachs in knots. We all breathed Professor Yang's name together, but it was Chou Chiang who showed himself to be the bravest of us all. He suddenly bristled, "Professor Yang has never said anything bad in class."

His father rose, furious. "Be quiet! If you say anything else, I'll give you a beating when we get home!"

My friend sat down, but the art teacher had already lost face in front of Chou Chiang's father. She bowed before him, shaking her head, like a dog before its master. "Forgive me, Officer Chou, it's my fault, I didn't inform them well enough. Do not be angry. I'll continue to drain the poison that Yang instilled in their minds."

"Yes, you're right, it's all your fault. You'd better reeducate them. This meeting doesn't satisfy me at all. We'll have to have another one."

In our opinion, the meeting ended perfectly — that is, in a shambles. Everyone left except Chou Chiang who was kept back by the art teacher. We all waited outside in the alley. In the end all she did was make him apologize to his father.

"Did she insult you?"

"No, she didn't dare, because it's thanks to my father that she is the new school principal."

"Is he going to beat you?"

"No way, my mother wouldn't let him."

Then we asked the head of our class if it was true that he had not written the denunciation himself and he said, yes, that was so. The art teacher had come to talk with his parents. "Since I was the class delegate, it was up to me to denounce Professor Yang. She left an essay with us that she had written. I didn't want to read it and it was my mother's idea to say that I didn't understand the characters."

We ended up appealing to Chou Chiang to persuade his father not to call another meeting. It did not take place, but neither did Professor Yang come back to school. They were saying she had committed suicide. That morning the children in our class came to school red-eyed, handkerchiefs in their hands.

One afternoon, Chou Chiang called to me, "Niu-Niu, do you want to see Professor Yang? This is no joke. They had a big meeting. Come on, follow me."

We ran, panting, to the abandoned theater.

We saw a figure sitting on a chair in the middle of the stage. We dashed towards it. It was our dear Professor Yang. She was motionless, impassive, her eyes closed and her skin white as paper. I wanted to look at her, but I was afraid at the same time to see the face that had given me so much love and happiness. She had changed so much, I could hardly recognize her.

"Professor Yang! Are you sleeping? It's me, Niu-Niu. Can you hear me? I came to see you. Wake up and I'll do whatever you tell me."

My throat grew tight. Chou Chiang, his whole body trembling, said, "Pardon me, Professor Yang, you know that I hate my father, that I hate myself. Professor Yang, are you coming back? All three of us, we'll go to the park again, won't we?"

Weeping uncontrollably, we were on our knees, our heads in her cold lap. Chou Chiang murmured, "Professor Yang is very cold." Without a word we tore down the political posters one by one and covered Professor Yang with them, so she was completely hidden. Then we sat next to her as we had when we watched the sunset on the river.

A few days later, rumor had it that the police were searching everywhere for those who had dared to tear down the posters and cover up the body of the criminal who had just undergone another session of criticism. We were pleased to hear that the police investigation was bogged down. For several nights after that, we continued to tear down posters in the street as our only way to avenge Professor Yang's death. We believed that she lived on the moon now and was satisfied with us as she looked down.

My grandmother had taught me that in this world there are eyes and hearts so unfailingly good that one day they will consume all that is bad in the world. I myself would also use my own heart to fight evil, for the sake of my grandfather, Mei Lin and her brother, and my very dear Professor Yang.

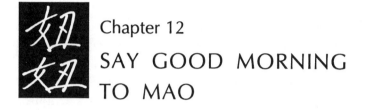

Chapter 12

SAY GOOD MORNING TO MAO

Summer arrived and school vacation. Other children went to the pool, but I couldn't go since I didn't have a swimsuit or the price of admission. So after helping my grandmother search through the garbage cans, I took a pail of water and splashed myself. I decided I had had as much fun as I would have had at the pool.

Chou Chiang invited me to go to the park with him. While we were there, he bought me an ice cream cone, a great luxury for me.

That same evening Grandmother Lei offered to take me to the country. One of her uncles had invited her to come help with the harvest and she would be sure to return with some produce. I had to beg my grandmother to let me go, because she was worried about it.

Two days later we were en route. I was jubilant at the idea of a stay in the country; my grandmother wept as she saw me off. We traveled in the back of a truck and then in a cart pulled by buffalo. The countryside beyond the town was magnificent — yellow, green, rust — all the crops were different colors as they ripened. Rice plants were yellow, corn was resplendent in green above the brown earth.

"Niu-Niu, you'll see, you'll have many friends. Everyone will be nice to you."

Grandmother Lei was right. As soon as we arrived at her uncle's place, the children, although they were bashful, seemed friendly. There were six of them, four boys and two girls. To celebrate our arrival, they had prepared a big dish of sweet potatoes and rice. I gulped down three full bowls, until my stomach couldn't hold any more.

This family lived in a house surrounded by bamboo in the midst of fields. A little stream flowed in front of their house. The six children and I soon became great friends. We all slept in the same bed where we had fun tickling each other and making a ruckus. During the day we searched for wild herbs and after cutting them up, gave them to the pigs to eat. We also helped the grown-ups tie up sheaves of rice. Our task was to pick up the stalks that had dropped, so as not to lose a single one. We found locusts that we grilled to eat; we also filched some of the neighbors' corn, until their children threatened us with sticks and chased us away. We ran along the river to elude them and plunged into the fresh water, then waited for the sun to set. At last it was time to search the fields with a torch, looking for frogs that we ate raw after peeling their skin and quickly cleaning them in the river.

We played without paying any attention to time until the call for supper — a wooden spoon struck against an old pot — reverberated from all the houses in the village. The old pot always hung outside and was also used to frighten off birds feeding on the crops.

Grandmother Lei said that I had put on weight and looked much healthier. I got to know all the children in the village. Since I came from the city, they asked me a thousand questions. Was it true that there were many cars and bicycles in the city, that houses had several floors? They also wanted to know what city folk looked like. Were they all as well dressed as I was? My miserable clothing seemed to them to be the finery of a princess. They asked me what good it did to know how to read and write. They seemed to be incredulous that I went to school, since in their area there was only one tiny school many miles away. Their parents considered their children's work in the fields more useful than sending them to school, since work meant food. These children therefore received no instruction at all.

I taught them a little reading and writing and they taught me the work in the fields. They nicknamed me "Professor Niu-Niu." Life seemed so sweet to me that I dreaded returning to the city.

One late afternoon we were bathing in the river when something drifted towards us. It was a baby in swaddling clothes. I screamed in shock. My friends made fun of me but I insisted that they find the infant's parents. They said that it was the parents who had thrown it into the water. A baby dead of hunger was a common sight for the farmers, but not to a young city-dweller like me. One of my playmates had lost his baby brother in the same way some months ago. His mother had promised to give him another. Here in the countryside people did not waste their time weeping.

The two weeks of vacation passed very quickly and again I climbed into the cart pulled by buffalo. For several miles my little friends followed us on foot up to the crossroads.

My grandmother bombarded me with questions about what we had done, how I felt about it all. "Tomorrow we'll go weigh you on the public scale to see how many pounds you've gained."

Two weeks later the schools reopened. All of us had to find

our way to a new school, where we would learn more of
Mao's sayings by heart and sing songs to his glory. The principal professor had added a new slogan to write: "Communism
is Great. Long Live Communism!"

I continued to take my studies seriously. I knew all the old
and the new citations by heart and cleaned the classroom
conscientiously.

A week after the opening of school, the professor announced that after we had chanted, "Good morning, Mao,"
we should all answer four questions every morning: "Do you
love Mao? Will you follow Mao all your life? Are you a good
child of Mao's? Do you have something to confess to Mao?"

For the first three questions, you had to answer without
hesitation. "Yes, I love the great Mao, I'll follow him all my
life. I'll do everything I can to be a good child of Mao." As
for the fourth, that was stickier. When the children had been
fighting or had not done their homework, they had to say,
"I have some faults to confess to Mao; yesterday I had a fight
with a friend . . . . I talked during class . . . . I ask Mao to pardon me and I ask all my classmates to forgive me, too. I will
improve immediately."

This was the ritual that took place every morning before
the lessons began. Even if we didn't understand everything,
we had to repeat the answers by heart, for Mao had said, *If
you understand, do better; if you don't understand, obey and understand later.*

That morning I joined in with the rest of the pupils who
answered in unison to the first questions. Then I added,
"Yesterday I finished my homework. I haven't fought with
anyone. I have nothing to confess to Mao. I'm a good child of
Mao."

"No, Niu-Niu! Especially not a good child of Mao!" the

professor said. "Think of what your parents are. Don't forget they're in a reeducation camp for the mistakes they've made. You must hate your parents and you do really have something to confess to Mao. Don't forget that you're the chief criminal. You're not a child of Mao!"

Every head turned in my direction, eyes staring at me, like knives cutting to the heart. I saw hatred in their eyes: I was reduced to less than nothing. Frantically I clasped my hands together, not knowing what to do. I wanted to justify myself, but no sound came from my lips. My vocal cords felt as though I were being choked. There was nothing to do but flee, yet my feet were glued to this floor. I hated that floor that offered me no hiding place.

"You have to write a self-criticism of your errors today!"

"I'd rather die than write that. You're a liar. My parents are working far away; they're not criminals. You're the bad one, you're the criminal!"

I hadn't finished when I was struck twice on the cheeks. I was so taken aback that I gulped with surprise. I looked at the professor with loathing, watching his mouth opening and closing and the hateful hand that had cuffed me. Suddenly an inner rage took hold of me, I lost my head, I couldn't stand it any more. I no longer could live like a stray dog. That hand waving in front of my face had killed my grandfather, had deported my parents. My heart broken, my lungs about to burst, shrieking, I suddenly threw myself at him, grabbing his hand so I could bite it. I put every ounce of strength into my teeth, grinding them to the bone.

Everyone was trying to restrain me, but I wasn't afraid and hung on until I could taste the professor's warm blood. Then I let go and spat in his face, my saliva mixed with blood and the exquisite taste of vengeance.

The other teachers threw me into a small, dark hold, and locked me in. I kicked the door, hit the wall with my fists, yelling. "You're liars! You killed my grandfather and sent away my parents. I know they're innocent! They're not criminals. Give me back my family! Give me back everything you stole!" I shrieked, I wept until my vocal chords were raw. I scratched the walls with my hands. I hit my back against the cement partition until I couldn't move. I was hoping that someone would come to open this terrible door, even to insult me; that at least someone would say something to me. I hoped for some pity. I didn't want to stay alone in the dark; they had isolated me like someone with the plague.

I was too exhausted to fight for a place in this perverse world. Finally, I collapsed onto the icy cement, staring at the ray of light under the door. My spirit had left my body and was wandering about in another world, like a leaf at the whim of the wind. There were flowers and sunshine over there, and birds and a lake. I allowed myself to drift lightly above the blue water among the freely moving clouds where there was not a living soul. That was all I wanted.

While I was having this daydream, the door was opened without my noticing it. Everything was white and empty. I couldn't remember anything.

Chou Chiang was waiting for me a short distance away, leaning against a tree. I needed to talk to him, just a word, but mechanically my feet took another direction. Nothing was real any more. My grandmother, my parents, seemed to be only another sordid part of this universe of lies. I hated this world into which I should never have been born, this chaos where I had no place.

The sun had disappeared below the horizon and the street lights had taken its place. Several farmers' carts gathering night-soil circulated in the streets. I wandered about without wanting to return home and fell asleep in a doorway.

When I opened my eyes again, a new, useless day had dawned. I found myself in my bed, my weeping grandmother watching over me. From her expression I understood that she knew what had happened. I loved her and hated her at the same time; I hated her for wounding me, for making me believe that my parents were working in some faraway place. I loved her because she loved me and because she was my grandmother.

I stayed in bed that whole day without moving, without eating. Afraid of returning to school, I tortured myself by repeating that my parents were criminals and that I was nothing but their despicable offspring. I was despised and had become a creature with no name. Not a human being, not an animal, but something as repugnant as a white maggot on rotten meat.

My grandmother washed the blood off my hand and placed a cold compress on my swollen eyelids. She looked after me from morning to evening, all the while wiping her eyes on her sleeve. If she was crying for me, she was wasting her time. In this society a tear was not worth anything. Why hadn't she gone to collect paper? I could then have lamented to my heart's content.

"Niu-Niu, I've made you some food. Eat a little, please."

I was really dying of hunger. I got up to go to the table. It was a bowl of white rice. It smelled so good that I bolted half of it down before I could even taste it. I noticed that her bowl had its usual sorry amount. The rice I had eaten suddenly became a heavy lump in my stomach. With a trembling hand, I pushed my bowl over to her, but she pushed it back to me. The bowl went back and forth several times, with both of us in tears.

"Grandmother, I . . ."

"Niu-Niu, don't say a word. You don't have to explain . . . I know everything. It's not your. . ." We were both overcome by emotion.

Two days later, my grandmother woke me before dawn to tell me that she was taking me back to school. I didn't say no. After the white rice, I was ready to do anything that she wanted. Even though education seemed to consist of writing entire pages of citations from Mao, my grandmother held to her firm belief that it was important for me to learn as many characters as possible.

She must have had to demean herself, to humiliate herself, to whine and beg on her knees to get the professor to agree to take me back. He demanded that when I went home I had to write my self-criticism to be read at the next meeting.

I faced my blank sheet of paper, blocked, unable to confess my faults. At a loss, my grandmother found only comforting words. "You must endure difficulties and shame and then let them go, unless you want to be as fragile as an eggshell that breaks on the rocks. Bamboo bends, it does not break. You must have confidence in yourself. Right now you are buffeted by the wind, but soon you'll regain your balance."

I gave in to Grandma because my love for her was greater than my hatred for the teacher. She was the strongest person I had ever known. Neither bereavement nor poverty had broken her. For me she endured humiliation and exhaustion. When I faltered, she encouraged me; when I gave up, she pushed me forward. I wrote two pages of self-criticism, most of which she dictated.

The day arrived and the principal addressed us. "Dear pupils, today the Revolution is making great strides. All the people are working hard and eagerly to build up our country. Everywhere the orioles warble and the swallows fly. In this atmosphere of universal cheer, our school must take a step forward, following the direction that Mao has shown us. Yet we have to be watchful, pay attention to bad influences that we must immediately correct and sweep away. In our school one of these bad influences has already struck. It was only last Tuesday that a student in the second year dared to attack a teacher! This pupil is named Niu-Niu. Her parents, counter-revolutionaries, detractors of Mao, are in a reeducation camp to accept the teaching of the masses. But she didn't understand the example of her parents. On Tuesday morning during the greeting to Mao, she committed a fault. The principal professor was kind enough to help her, but she insulted him, even going so far as to bite him.

"This, dear pupils, is intolerable. Our professors have done everything to reeducate her. Now the criminal will read her self-criticism so that we may correct her faults. Listen to her."

After this long string of lies, my hatred rose up again. I wanted once more to shriek out my innocence, but for the love of my grandmother, for the comfort she had given me, this time I got hold of myself. Gritting my teeth, I walked to the podium. I looked out over a sea of black heads, while next to me the professor watched me contemptuously. I wasn't afraid, I found this whole situation ridiculous, very funny, like some enormous farce. Why were they all here, wasting their time on me?

Gradually I unfolded my paper, which had been corrected by the professor. I then recited the list of my sins and offered repentance. "Dear Professors, dear classmates, I am now solemnly going to confess before you. Tuesday morning, while Professor Wang was so kindly teaching me, I used vicious words against him. Yet he didn't become angry, but continued to talk to me patiently. Refusing to listen, however, I was stubborn and bit him to the bone. Then the other professors came in to help him control me. What is more, I insulted them too, and tore their clothes.

"My shortcomings are very serious, they are unpardonable. I am ashamed, but I beg you nevertheless to continue helping me correct my faults. My mistakes show that I have not understood the aim of the great Cultural Revolution and that I don't have enough love for Mao. All my life I must study Mao's sayings with determination and love the Party with all my heart and . . . ."

Finally I finished reading my long speech which I didn't completely understand myself and returned to my place.

To help mend my ways, I had to clean the room where the meeting had been held. In fact, I amused myself by twirling the huge broom around me. In any case, this place was never clean. Since I had to do this for a whole week, I wasn't going to tax myself.

Suddenly Chou Chiang came toward me. We hadn't seen each other for a week.

"Niu-Niu, do you want me to help you?"

"No, it's for me to do. It's my punishment."

"Niu-Niu, is it true that your parents — "

"Yes, they're in prison. What else do you want? You want to know how my grandfather died? Yes, he was a criminal and I'm the child of criminals!" I didn't want him to pity me the way that one feels sorry for a stray cat. "My parents aren't as high up as your father, the leader of the Red Guards."

Having told him everything, I felt all my strength drain

away. I sat down on the ground, thinking that Chou Chiang would never speak another word to me. I didn't dare look at him — I dreaded hearing his receding footsteps. But instead I heard his beautiful words that were a balm to my heart.

"Niu-Niu, I know it's not your fault. We're good friends, right? I have faith in you."

My tears of happiness washed away my humiliation. He took a piece of paper out of his bag and I lent him my pen so that he could solemnly write two lines: "I swear never to leave Niu-Niu and if I don't keep my promise, may I turn into a dog." I still wanted him to put his fingerprint in red ink on it. Since none was on hand, we both spat on a propaganda poster against which he pressed his fingers before leaving his imprint on his oath.

"With five fingers it counts for more."

I carefully put the piece of paper in the inside pocket of my vest (and have kept it ever since). The two of us continued to sweep the courtyard and to burn the trash.

"Niu-Niu, did you know that in Tibet they dance around the fire?"

He then taught me the fire-dance. You had to shout and jump energetically. Chou Chiang had made me forget the fire that raged within me.

Starting the following Monday, when we greeted Mao, I had to say, "Great Mao, I am at fault. Because of my family, I am a criminal child. I will try to improve and do whatever you order me to do."

This kept up until the professor tired of it. He put me in a corner in the rear of the classroom, as though I were a dummy, and never spoke to me. When I raised my hand to answer, he never called on me. My homework was considered worthless, no longer even worth correcting. My name was mentioned only as a dreadful example. "If you continue to do badly, the same thing will happen to you that happened to Niu-Niu. You'll be banished to the back of the room and you'll have to confess publicly at school assembly."

Now my back was to the wall. I didn't care about anything. It had to be true that I deserved my bad name. I no longer studied. I grew careless in cleaning the classroom.

My classmates completely ignored me. That was just as well, because I had nothing to say to them. If they did call me names, I went one better. The hoodlums whom I knew from the streets had taught me how to behave in the very worst way. It was simpler to really *be* bad. Chou Chiang alone remained unconditionally loyal to me.

Chapter 13

PAPER HANDCUFFS

The neighbors on our little street were people of modes means. They earned their livelihood by gathering up chunk of coal or making shoes from cloth. They had to live ver frugally.

We had lived here for three years. Some ten years ear lier, the place had been a public rubbish dump. Following an earthquake, tenants in apartment houses that had been damaged moved here and built small wood cabins. Since the apartment houses had not actually collapsed, the tenants had eventually deserted their makeshift living quarters to return to them. Peasants seeking work had succeeded them. They protected the cabins from the wind by covering them with a mixture of wet sand, fine yellow earth and coal. Little by little, they planted trees along the small street and, having succeeded in getting rid of the dump, they gave the street a name that expressed their hopes: Treasure Street.

These last years, the street had become famous. Hadn't Mao said, *The poorer you are, the more honorable. The poorer you are, the more revolutionary?*

The most recent arrivals were like us, people who had "committed mistakes" or who belonged to the wrong class. Chased from their homes, they had been relocated on the poorest, most miserable streets in order to "accept the conditions of

the working class and the criticism of the masses."

Sometimes, however, events take an unexpected turn. After a long period of living side by side and with everyone working desperately just to survive, no one had the leisure to torment us any longer. On the contrary, we became friendly with our old accusers, because we, the bad elements of society, knew how to read and write and they often came to us for help in writing or reading their letters. During festivities we did the calligraphy that customarily adorned doors. That was how my grandmother had come to read Grandmother Lei the letter from her grandson. There was, of course, an official City Committee that kept an eye on everyone's actions, but the atmosphere was somewhat better in the neighborhood: all of us dressed in Mao blue were in the same boat.

Often some men, a yoke slung over their shoulders — bellows dangling from one side and a little oven from the other — would come down our small street, calling out, "Popcorn! Popcorn!" Since none of us could afford candy, cake or fruit, popcorn was our only treat, though Grandma bought it very seldom. I would watch the others bringing their corn to have it popped and, like the other kids, grab whatever fell into the sand. We swallowed them just like that, before anyone could take them away from us. That is how I came to make the acquaintance of Chin Yen, the only girl in a gang of the poorest and hungriest boys.

Because her house was close to mine, we became good friends. She was four years older than I. Her parents worked in a large textile mill, her mother at the machines, her father in the office. Her younger brother was called Jinguo. The inside of their house, though much bigger than ours, was practically empty: one table that served all sorts of purposes, one large cupboard and a single bed where the adults slept on one

side, the children on the other, facing in the opposite direction.

Her parents spoke very little, but were touchingly kind. They would offer me a nut, a piece of corn bread, a few grilled peas or popcorn.

Chin Yen told me about their life. Her father had been a farmer. Thanks to the village chief, he had been able to enter the Workers and Farmers University where he studied in order to become a professor himself. He began to teach a class nearby. Most children, however, were kept at home by their parents so that they could work in the fields. Her father had succeeded in attracting only three students, but it was a start. Unfortunately, some time later the kindly village chief was replaced by another who was completely hostile to education and the school was closed.

Chin Yen's father was banished to the city to find work. At the outset he worked at the machines, but since propaganda for the Cultural Revolution required the writing of posters and he was literate, he was transferred to the factory office.

For the New Year's festivities, always celebrated with great excitement in honor of one's ancestors, Chin Yen's family would return to their village to visit the grandparents and uncles. It was traditional to kill a pig and roast it whole. Of course, the best parts — feet, head and entrails — went to the village chief.

Naturally, the chance to eat pork aroused my greed and I was in a hurry to become a peasant. When my new friend's father invited me to spend the next New Year's celebrations with them, I was as ready to leave as an arrow from a taut bow. Yet it was important not to visit Chin Yen's family too often, so as not to cause them trouble. Even though we might forget that we were known as criminals, someone else would remember it for us.

Since Chin Yen's father had the same family name as my grandmother, she told me to call him Uncle Wang. He encouraged his daughter and me to be close friends and make up whenever we quarreled, with the older yielding to the younger. He would join our hands together to pledge our true friendship.

Finally, winter came and the New Year approached that would take me into the country to feast on pork meat. One morning I saw a strange sight from the window; it frightened me so much I shouted for my grandmother.

"That's snow, Niu-Niu. You've never seen it before. Isn't it interesting? It's like in the story of the little match girl." She explained that it had been many years since it had been this thick on the ground. Perhaps it was because the Year of the Tiger was beginning. "White snow purifies everything. Next year we'll be lucky."

It was the first time I had seen real snow and it was as though I were living a fairy tale. I hadn't imagined that it could transform the place into a magnificent city. On the sidewalks, the trees, the roofs, the crystals lay like diamonds. And the snow brought new fun with it: you could make a snowman and then hit it with snowballs; the snow provided free ice cream too!

When my grandmother was young, her family would pay a group of traveling players to put on *Snow in June*, an opera that told the story of a young girl who was beheaded as a result of a judicial error. Before she died, she said that even the skies would be downcast because of the injustice she had suffered, so she prayed for the snow to fall in summer. She was taken for a madwoman, but her death was followed by a devastating June blizzard that howled for three days. Though lamentations filled the glacial air, the snow killed only the judge who had sentenced her and those who had made fun of her.

My grandmother's story convinced me that we owed the snow covering the city to the ghost of someone who had suffered an injustice.

One day I went to Chin Yen's house to invite her to a snowball fight, but the door was locked, as it was on the days following. Had they left for the country already? But Uncle Wang had promised to take me! Perhaps they were afraid I would eat too much pork . . . .

Two days before the New Year, my grandma had purchased some firecrackers, so I could scare away bad spirits and welcome the New Year of the Tiger. I left the house, hoping to find Chin Yen at home. Together we would shoot off firecrackers and continue our friendly squabbling.

The padlock was undone. Through the opening I could see my friend alone inside. I was happy; they hadn't left without me after all.

"Chin Yen, It's me — Niu-Niu!"

But she didn't budge an inch. I could see only her back.

"Chin Yen, let me in! I have good news to tell you."

She didn't move. Perhaps she couldn't hear me. Maybe she was sulking because of my family? She'd known about me from the start!

"Chin Yen, what's the matter? If I've done anything bad, tell me. I'll change. We're good friends. Why don't you open the door?"

At last she turned around. She was crying. "Niu-Niu, don't come see me any more. It's not because of you, it's my father — the stable — go! I'll come and see you."

She burst into tears. I tried my best to calm her, but it was no use so I decided to come back again the next day.

I shot off my firecrackers all by myself and then walked about, looking at the meat drying outside the houses. I hoped that her father was not at the "stable" — a sort of private prison, where village bosses were known to put resisters who could stay there for years thinking about their mistakes. Such prisons were called "stables" because Mao had nicknamed the intellectuals "demons of the cow," alluding to the evil genies of Chinese mythology. The expression was later reduced to "cows" and applied to all categories of Revisionists. So, naturally, wherever they were imprisoned was called a "stable."

My grandmother expected the worst, even though this involved a decent man who didn't seem to have done anything wrong. We went together to see Mrs Wang. Yes, her husband had indeed been assigned to the stable. She was normally taciturn, but the words came flowing out of her.

"We obviously have serious problems. We would never have imagined that they would dredge up an old incident. Years ago, my husband went to Beijing for a meeting. He took the opportunity to buy me some flower seeds that I wanted. Several days later, at the same seed store, the police arrested a spy whose contact was supposedly a very thin man wearing glasses. In checking out all the customers on that fateful day, they came upon my husband who is very thin, but who does not wear glasses! Besides, how could a villager be a spy? Anyway, the mistake was straightened out in Beijing. You know us, Grandmother Liu — we're peaceable, discreet people. We've never interfered in things that don't concern us. We worked like everyone else at the factory, following the director's orders to the letter, doing what we were supposed to do. All we wanted was a peaceful life and to be provided with what we needed. My husband knew how to read and write, so he left the machines to work in the office. That was a promotion — his salary didn't go up, but his fellow workers were jealous. A week ago during a meeting at the factory, an envious co-worker brought up the spy story; he said that my husband had come here to hide out. That's the reason he's in jail without any evidence against him and why he's forced to write a self-critical autobiography."

"But why didn't you tell them to look at the results of the initial inquiry? They must be on file somewhere."

"They treat us as liars and we're going to end up being considered real spies. My husband told me not to make a fuss. The chief has formally forbidden us to see him until the problem is resolved."

"Maybe we could be of some help to you, Mrs Wang — take something to him perhaps?"

She reacted to our offer with fear. "They would never agree to it."

"Grandma, why don't they try to see him at night? There aren't very many guards and I heard that one could arrange it with them."

"No, they can't do that," Grandmother said. "They're wearing paper handcuffs."

I didn't understand. "Yes," Mrs Wang said, "we have invisible handcuffs, handcuffs as fragile as paper."

"If you can't see them, if they're as fragile as paper, why can't you tear them up?"

"It isn't that simple," my grandmother said. "For hundreds of years people have lived in fear and it is that fear that people call paper handcuffs. Children fear their parents, students fear their teachers, wives fear their husbands and people fear their governors and the emperor. Everyone follows tradition. Everyone says we must endure our bitter lives — that's the price of survival. If people are defiant and speak out, their heads roll as they open their mouths. In the old days, it was the rebels who suffered the consequences. If the action was against the emperor, as many as a thousand people might be killed in reprisal. At least nowadays it's not so savage, families are separated but not always destroyed. They separate the wife from the husband, friends, children. But your father and your grandfather were too outspoken — "

"Grandma, do you wear paper handcuffs?"

"Yes, and they are very heavy."

"But I don't want handcuffs. If they're made of paper, I'll burn them."

"You're like your father and grandfather, Niu-Niu. Your blood is hot: I'm afraid for you. You're bright and lovable, but I don't want you to get into trouble."

So unless I lived a lie, I would not receive the roses my grandfather had promised me? Well, I no longer wanted them. When would the day come that the emperor would no longer bind his people with paper handcuffs?

I was convinced that the snow falling that night was meant to avenge unhappy people. It would make the whole world white and clean, I thought. These immaculate snowflakes were falling for us.

 Chapter 14

IN A BAD WAY

The snow did not turn out to be as beneficial as my grandma had predicted. On the contrary, the Year of the Tiger brought catastrophe. South China lost its harvest that year. Rural people were driven from their villages by hunger, and took refuge in the city to beg. In the streets children could be heard crying and the pleas of women rang through the city: "Help our children, give us some food! They are the only ones left, the others are dead. I beg you to give us something." Peasants ate leaves and bark off the trees. In the city the rats were eaten next and then the paste used for the propaganda posters (a serious crime against the Revolution).

I had grown up in poverty, in a damp cabin open to the four winds and I had innumerable oozing sores on my skin, but we had no money to buy medicine. Once at a great sacrifice we bought some salve, but it only made my skin worse. Occasionally a kindly neighbor gave us some tincture of iodine and Grandma painted my back. My skin burned horribly. The worst was the nightly itching. I scratched myself till I bled, so that the pus flowed, but the torment continued. Repulsive red and yellow stains covered my bedding and clothes. My grandmother was helpless. She gathered wild herbs far outside the city to concoct traditional remedies, but nothing worked.

I was ashamed to dry my blanket on the street in full view

of everyone. I preferred to hang it in the little court behind the cabin, but my precautions were in vain. Children in the street and at school coined horrible nicknames for me — "abscess," "garbage can," "moldy skin," "snake skin." They liked to spit at me and pull my hair. When I couldn't stand it any longer, I hit back. Luckily, I was strong from having helped my grandmother carry bundles of paper and I knew how to hurt. But I felt helpless most of the time, especially since I was afraid of getting expelled from school — that would be the final blow to my grandmother's hopes. So I acted indifferent, as though I didn't hear them. This made them throw even more stones and trash at me.

Chou Chiang defended me. "If anyone says bad things to Niu-Niu, I'll sock him one and ask my father to set up a criticism session." His childish threats actually stopped them. I couldn't imagine that his father, whom I hated, would ever protect me. That would have been one of life's more questionable ironies!

I had always loved summer, playing in water during the dog days. Now I abhorred this season. As long as I could stand it, I would wear long sleeves that made me sweat and made my boils itch horribly. Whenever I uncovered myself and others looked at me, I felt as if an electric charge were going through me. The dresses from my childhood had gradually disintegrated until only the gift from Professor Yang remained on the shelf.

The general mood was growing bleak. All everyone talked about was the struggle against "efforts to cancel the Cultural Revolution." At home, our bouillon became thinner and thinner. My stomach was constantly growling and every morning I left for school feeling weak.

One day after class I lingered in the street looking for something to eat. The sounds and enticing smells escaping from the restaurant kitchens and back courts made my mouth water. The displays of food taunted me, making me dizzy. Who was going to eat all this food? I didn't ask much. A little bit of corn bread would have satisfied me. I dreamed of becoming a queen who would sit enthroned on a mountain of meat to nibble as she pleased until her belly was as swollen as a pregnant woman's.

When I came upon a display of *pao tzu* rolls, it danced before my eyes, mocking me as in a dream. I took one and ran. It was so hot in my hand, I could smell how delicious it was going to be. Behind me they were yelling, "Catch her!" I ran fast, the wind whistling in my ears. I lost my way, coming up against a wall. I put the *pao tzu* in my pocket and clinging with hands and feet, I climbed over the huge obstacle. Buddha helped me; I managed to jump to the other side. Without taking time to get up, I gulped down my *pao tzu* in three swallows. Now they could catch me! But no one came. I wiped my mouth and rose. It was only then that I realized that I had taken a bad fall. My backside hurt. The heck with it! I'd fall ten more times for this little roll!

Limping, I returned home, soothing my grandmother's worries with lies. Unfortunately, my success gave me a taste for stealing. I began to filch everything within my reach, not only food, but also washing hung out in the street which I sold to an itinerant ragman for a few pennies to be spent on food.

The inevitable happened when I was caught stealing five fens. The police took me home, where they slapped me hard, showing my grandmother the money to shame her. "Bring her up better than that!"

They left me to my grandmother who was speechless. She made me stand in front of her, but consumed by guilt, I couldn't look her in the eye.

"It's not true, is it? They're not being fair to you?"

She had such confidence in me. I felt worse than if she had slapped me. I kept my head lowered.

"Niu-Niu, my dear child, forgive me. I don't give you enough to eat. I'll try to look for more paper in the trash cans and make more matchboxes . . ."

"I stole, Grandma. They told the truth. I'm a thief."

I didn't have the courage to stay there for another second; I went out to find some dark corner to lie in. I was sure my grandmother would hate me from that day on. I had betrayed her, she who washed my clothes, cooked, worked like a beast of burden for me and always gave me most of the food. I sat on the sidewalk cursing myself until nightfall. I heard her calling down the street, but I didn't dare return.

When midnight struck, I was exhausted, staggering with fatigue, and decided to go home. The light was out. I opened the door quietly and by the moonlight I could see that Grandma was sleeping. It was better that way. I slipped under the covers, but my skin was itching.

"Niu-Niu, not so hard. It's bad again, isn't it?" Of course she wasn't sleeping. She never went to sleep until I was in bed. I waited, fearing she would start talking, but all I heard was the sound of rats gnawing at the wood.

Days passed. Grandma really was working much harder than before, because the soup was now somewhat less thin. One day coming back from school, I found her lying on the bed, looking ill. I approached her immediately, touching her on the forehead just as she always touched me.

"Grandma, what's the matter? Are you sick?"

"No, it's not serious . . . . There's some money under the

bed. Buy yourself something to eat."

That was too much. Even when she was seriously ill, she worried about me.

I ran to Grandmother Lei's house for help. To her, Grandma admitted she felt faint and her heart was beating very fast.

"You have to eat, Mrs Liu! You're sick from hunger!"

The money under the bed was only enough to buy a piece of corn bread, while she needed rice and meat. I knew that if Grandmother Lei had something better to propose, she would already have done it. This time I went out to steal for my grandmother. It was immoral, but necessary.

I used that money to buy some rice and two eggs to make a bowl of soup. She looked at me strangely and asked where I had found this feast. I lied and said it was Chin Yen's mother who had given me the food.

"But they don't have much either. They're very kind."

I told her that I had already eaten over there.

The next day she was a bit better, which gave me comfort. A little later, however, she reproached me for lying.

"Niu-Niu, this will have been the last, won't it? I'm not angry, because I know you did it for the love of me. But promise me that you won't start again."

"It's true, Grandma, that I don't want to be a thief. Everytime I steal, I get scared. I swear to you I won't do it again."

But I did not keep my promise. Gradually, without a conscious effort, I had developed a terrible habit. My grandmother threatened to commit suicide to force me to change, but this was the only way I could help her: she herself had gone beyond her strength, her feet had wandered down too many city streets, her hands had put together too many matchboxes.

Despite her efforts, we were hungry and sick. I didn't understand why some people were able to eat their fill and dress well. We didn't work any less than they did. Why didn't we have a right to the minimum for survival? I found it unbearable that my grandmother should be growing weaker by the hour and ever nearer to drawing her last breath. She had brought me up and now it was my turn to do something for her. I had made up my mind to steal and I couldn't go back on that.

I went to buy cornmeal and oil which I mixed with our provisions. If I got caught, I could stand the insults, and I could even stand the blows better than I could bear hunger. I was careful to wipe the blood off my mouth before coming home. I did my dirty job properly, avoiding our own neighborhood.

One day, while I was hiding some money in Grandma's envelope, she came in without warning. With rising anger, she threw down what she held in her hand. Catching me by the collar, she yelled, "Go put the money back where you stole it from! Are you too big to obey these days? You're bad! I've wasted my strength and my hopes on you." Throwing the money in my face, she continued furiously, "Take it back! I prefer death to touching this rotten money!"

"Oh good! Even if you die, no one will admit that you were honest! For them, we're already criminals. I want to steal and I'll kill if I have to. They don't deny themselves, so why should I? I'll steal as long as I live!"

Before I finished, she was hitting me in the face. Surprised, I began to howl like an animal. "Very good! Beat me! Do you know that I can't stand you? I hate all of you, including those two who were my parents! It's because of you that people can hit me and humiliate me. And they've done everything but take my clothes off in public!"

My grandmother was pulling at her hair, covering her face

with her hands, all the while shrieking. But I didn't care and continued to shout, finding so many mean things to say that I surprised myself. God knows how one can hurt those one loves.

"Why are you crying? Because I've become a thief or because my skin is so repulsive? I want to cry too, but I have no tears for you. Nobody pays any attention to us, and from now on we're not going to have anything to do with each other. I'd rather be an orphan thrown in the river than stay with you."

My grandmother had collapsed on the floor, an arm extended toward me, dragging herself on her knees. "Niu-Niu, what are you saying? You're raving." She wanted to take me in her arms, but I pushed her away, repeating that I hated her and that I didn't want her to touch me. I finished by slapping her, hard.

The earth began to heave. She put her hand up to her reddened face. I was stupefied, aghast. I began to tremble terribly, my hand that I had raised against my grandmother burning like fire. How could I have struck my own grandmother? No, it wasn't me, it was someone else!

Suddenly I felt my grandmother's breath on my hand, softly kissing it. My hand had become like the claw of an animal. I wanted to talk to her, to cry out, to call my grandma, but I felt completely weak, as though I were about to faint. A soft murmur came to my ears.

"My little Niu-Niu, I know that you didn't mean to . . ."

Hot tears clouded my sight. My guilt sank in and I heard myself stammering, "Grandma, my grandma . . . I need you so much . . ."

Then I collapsed at my grandmother's feet. Her sweet words reached me as though I were in a fog.

"Niu-Niu, I'm here for you. I love you. You're everything

to me. I'll always be with you. We'll be fine, the two of us."

I shivered. "Hit me, Grandma. Hit me hard. Please, beat me!"

My grandmother's tears, more precious than gold to me, made me swear I would never steal again and if I did, I would cut off my arms and legs. In spite of my poverty and hunger, I would follow my grandmother's example and grit my teeth.

Each time that greed overcame me, I gave myself a violent slap. Each time my hands reached out to take something, I bit them till I bled. All this rather than hurt my grandma.

 **Chapter 15**

WHO AM I?

To please my grandmother, I began again to study assiduously. She taught me this poem of Li Po:

> You don't see the waters of the Yellow River
> As it rolls from the heavens to the sea.
> You don't see the mirror in the great hall
> Reflecting your sad, white hair that looks
> Like blue silk threads in the morning light,
> But like snow in the evening.
> When life smiles on you, follow your happiness
> To the end. Do not leave empty under the moon
> Your golden cup. If heaven has ordained
> My talent, let me use it, even if it means
> The loss of a thousand gold pieces.
> One day they will return to me.

It was mysterious, but comforting.

"You see, Niu-Niu, the great poets also had their moments of misery and unhappiness, but they knew how to overcome them. I'm sure that you have the same ability."

Following her advice, I wrote in my diary before going to bed. She would correct my errors and I would recopy it in another notebook that she had bought for this purpose.

Today I wrote: "I haven't seen Chin Yen for a long time. Uncle Wang is still confined to the stable. Grandma doesn't know when he'll be free. Yesterday I heard Grandmother Lei say that Chin Yen was running around with hoodlums. I can't believe it."

My grandma praised me for my writing. She gave me permission to go see Chin Yen just as long as I avoided her bad friends. I had a hard time understanding how anyone could be worse than a child of criminals.

Grandmother had reason to worry. The city was sliding into chaos. Many people were sleeping in the streets where, day after day, Red Guards went parading.

At school everyone had to carry a wooden gun to act out the killing of criminals and enemies. The teacher would take us to the movies to see the official films which played during the Cultural Revolution. The stories were all the same: they showed how the people had found their enemies or how the Red Army had won the war. The movies were compulsory and I had to deprive myself of food to pay for my ticket. Everywhere there were propaganda posters against American imperialism, against Khrushchev, against whatever . . . . Although we did not understand them, we were obliged to shout out slogans with the adults. In this hysterical atmosphere, I turned nine years old.

Chin Yen introduced me to Ta-Chün, a sixteen-year-old who lived in the suburbs in a tiny shack behind a factory. "Welcome to our gang. Chin Yen told me that your parents had their problems and were taken away. And she told me that at school they give you trouble." He acted like a party boss in the movies. "I've decided to help you. Tomorrow you'll show us who's bothering you, so we can punch them in the face."

"But why do you want — "

"I only accept people into my gang who are having a hard time. That way we can help each other."

Sure enough, the next morning Ta-Chün, my new friend, came with two buddies to beat up the kid I pointed out after warning him and threatening him with more of the same if he did not stop bothering me. Ta-Chün had given me back my self-respect.

Chin Yen, who was the only one who knew it, told me Ta-Chün's story. His parents were soldiers in the Red Army. They had been beaten to death during the Cultural Revolution and his own brother had belonged to the gang of killers. Ta-Chün had followed him until this notorious band was destroyed by the army. He had escaped, but his brother had been sentenced to fifteen years in prison. Ever since, Ta-Chün lived alone, stealing his food.

I came to know the other members of the gang. There was Tien Yeh, a boy of thirteen. His parents were musicians; when he was nine, his mother had been taken away. His father decided to divorce her and "stop all contact with criminals." Tien Yeh preferred to live in poverty with his sister rather than ask for help from his father, whom they could never forgive. The director of the Conservatory of Music had come to advise his sister to renounce their mother. When she refused to do it, the father didn't want to see her again and he remarried.

"One day, when we were quarelling, my sister and I broke a magnificent trophy my mother had won for acting. My sister cried as she picked up the pieces and we decided, in our mother's memory, to stop fighting."

All by himself, Tien Yeh studied painting, the only thing that counted for him from then on. His sister worked in a factory to earn their living and pay for his art supplies.

All of us had tortured family histories, but when we were together, no one ever asked questions. If someone felt the need to talk about his unhappiness, he did it spontaneously.

There was one girl of my own age in the group. A Ch'iao was her name and she too was covered with pustules, which reinforced our friendship. Her parents had been professors in the university and were also incarcerated in a stable. Her brothers had been sent to the countryside to be "reeducated through labor." She had lived with an aunt, a cruel woman who had exploited her as a servant, going so far as to beat her and force her to sleep in the basement. A Ch'iao had run away.

We were a dozen kids all in the same boat. Our leader organized everything we did. During the day we fought with rival gangs and stole our food from factories and stores. In the evening we went out to tear down propaganda posters or throw stones at apartment house windows until the occupants came out and called us names. Then we ran off, whistling.

They taught me how to pick pockets. You had to learn to rub the index against the middle finger to make them supple and strong, so that you could slip them into the pockets of passersby without their noticing. When we saw people on the street carrying purses, it didn't matter whether they carried them on their left or their right. We followed them until they came to an area where there were fewer people. Then we gave them a hard pinch on the elbow — you had to find the exact spot on the person's tendon — so they wouldn't feel anything for a minute. This gave the thief time to grab the purse and pass it on to an accomplice without the victim being aware of what was happening.

In the bus our pickpocketing required four people. First, we spotted the best-dressed person, one who had bulging pockets. One of us watched the other passengers while the others surrounded the mark to shield him from observation. We had to work each side to search all the pockets. If one of us got caught, the three others did not run away, but stayed to take the punishment with him. When we were successful, the law of the group was that we celebrated at a restaurant, eating and drinking.

The first time that I received five maos as my part of the spoils, I bought a present for Chou Chiang — a small notebook as a token of our friendship. He was in seventh heaven, although he didn't understand how I could have afforded to buy it. I fooled him by telling him that I had found some little job.

We had pinched a large wallet which had five yuans in it, a fortune to us. While the boys went to buy things for our feast, the girls prepared the bowls, the chopsticks, and set out the glasses of liquor. In the middle of the meal, to our general stupefaction, Ta-Chün announced his marriage to Chin Yen. Tien Yeh was offended that they had dispensed with their parents' consent. Ta-Chün himself didn't know why they were getting married, a joke perhaps, to imitate the adults and maybe because society had outlawed us and we needed to create a new society of our own: children of criminals, the country's outcasts.

Our ritual at the meal followed what we had seen in a movie: we raised our glasses in a toast: *A fun wedding makes a happy marriage!* Chin Yen had now been elevated to "big sister."

We often talked about our plans for the future. Tien Yeh wanted to become a great painter, Chin Yen wanted to be a waitress in a restaurant so she could nibble while she was working, Ta-Chün wanted to be a soldier to kill all the bad guys with his rifle. He was the only one who would know them for what they were . . . . As for me, I wanted to be a teacher in honor of Professor Yang. However, they didn't want me to leave the gang, because I had a good technique.

When I returned in the evening, I lied to my grandmother so she wouldn't worry, saying that I'd spent the evening with Chin Yen or hung around outside Uncle Wang's stable.

Some time after the "marriage" I asked Chin Yen to tell me what had changed in her relationship with Ta-Chün. She blushed to the roots of her hair and I had a hard time getting her to talk. She admitted to me that Ta-Chün had read in a sex manual that a husband must touch his wife's breasts. When I asked her what was so special about her breasts, she answered, "Nothing. They're somewhat like yours except that when one is married, they should be caressed."

I thought to myself that if I married Chou Chiang, he would touch my breasts. I wanted to know if Ta-Chün was nice to her or if he beat her.

"Yes, twice now, but that's normal. My father beat my mother when he was angry."

I hoped that Chou Chiang would spare me, but if he felt like it, I'd let him do it. I'd never seen Chou Chiang hit anyone, so I was curious to see what would happen.

"You know, Niu-Niu, that Ta-Chün is really very nice. The first time I saw him he acted so macho and tough, but I found out before long that this was just an act he put on; he was playing the leader."

Later I asked my grandmother why a husband had to touch his wife's breasts. She seemed embarrassed, calling me all kinds of names. "I forbid you to say such stupid things. If you do, you'll get slapped."

I confessed that I had learned that from Chin Yen, but I shouldn't have, for my grandmother, instead of calming down, went straight down the street to my friend's house. Poor Chin Yen! Standing outside, I could hear her cries and weeping. Through the opening of the door I could see her kneeling on the washboard, holding out her hands to the blows from the bamboo switch. Her mother seemed beside herself.

I was ashamed of myself, certain that I had made a terrible mistake. Otherwise the adults would not be so angry with her. That taught me a lesson; I would have to be more careful about confiding in my grandmother.

One day when we were prepared to pass Ta-Chün a large pocketbook pinched on the bus, we noticed an old woman sobbing in a small crowd of people. She sat, striking her head and hands on the ground, lamenting that her money had been stolen. "My son is in the hospital and this money was lent to me under oath by peasant friends. My son is in danger. I beg of you, give me back my money!"

My mouth was dry. It was disgusting of us to have taken her cash. On a moment's impulse, and without knowing if it really belonged to her, I said, "Grandmother, perhaps this is it. I found it over there."

I left, running as fast as I could. Her thanks, called after me, broke my heart. "Thank God. Thank you, my benefactress, thank you."

I continued to run. I kept seeing her grey eyes overflowing with tears. I didn't want to steal. I had no right to go on like this. At the beginning it had been a lark, just fun. Now I had been made aware of my loathsomeness: I had become a real delinquent.

Ta-Chün was not angry. He said I could stop stealing, provided that I stayed a member of the gang. Our friendship remained unshakable. A feast paid for by our leader's own money marked the end of my activity.

One autumn in 1976, the weather was so bad that the sky seemed about to fall in on us. I was going to school as usual, but something strange was in the air. There was silence. It seemed that the bicycles had lost their bells and people's faces looked serious. Fleetingly, I thought of July's earthquake at Tangshun that had killed a million people.

The class was less noisy than usual as I squeezed myself into my seat. The professor hadn't arrived yet, while the loudspeaker was broadcasting funeral music as it had upon Chou En Lai's death. Finally the professor came in, his eyes brimming with tears. Before going to his desk, he looked at us with deep sadness, taking a terribly long time before uttering a sound, as though tears were choking him.

"Dear pupils! I have a real calamity to announce. Our . . . great . . . our great star, our benefactor, President Mao, has left us for a long time." He stopped and collapsed into his chair, sobbing.

The pupils looked at one another. After we had filled our notebooks with "Long Life to Mao," how could he possibly die? If he really was dead, it meant we no longer had the red sun nor a helmsman. What would become of us? We had wished him life for a thousand years repeatedly, just as in earlier times they had wished that for emperors, my grandma had told me.

The principal's voice came over the loudspeaker, drowning out the moans of the teacher.

"Dear pupils! We are going to cancel classes for three days

while we mourn our great President Mao. We shall make white paper flowers and funeral wreaths for an assembly this afternoon. Everyone must wear a black armband." He too wept into the microphone.

That morning, for the first time since I had started school, we had not said good morning to Mao. Without ceasing to weep, the professor had us cut out paper flowers. At first a few in the class also cried, then the whole class joined in. The whole school was sincere in its despair. I hadn't wept because I was too hungry, not having had anything to eat that morning. But I was sad too.

They put our flowers on the windows, the doors and around Mao's portrait. The pupils had to fasten one to their right sleeve, and put the armband on the left, before assembling in the courtyard that afternoon. We were quieter and better behaved than we had ever been before.

On the podium a huge portrait of Mao, surrounded by flowers and large black characters, hung over some potted conifers. After a long moment of silence, the principal addressed us in a low voice. "Stand up. Let us show Mao our deep sadness. We will bow three times." Then he asked us to observe three minutes of silence, signaled by an interruption in the music coming from the loudspeakers. Everyone stood straight as a stick, but with head bowed.

The sound of weeping made heaven and earth tremble. In this macabre atmosphere, even *my* eyes were wet. All my education had centered on Mao and I knew nothing higher than him. He was good, he was the founder of the new China and without him our own existence would have amounted to nothing. He was the symbol of everything: the sun, the father, the star of salvation. In weeping over his sad fate, I bitterly regretted that my parents had committed errors against him and I was disappointed that I myself had not had time to complete my reeducation to become one of his good children — a good child of Mao.

After the school had finished its outpouring of emotion, the principal asked us to raise our right fist to swear that our heart belonged to Mao, repeating the words, "Our adored Mao, our red sun, we are sad to be mourning for you. You continue to live in your eternal sleep. It is not only a calamity for our country, but for the whole world. Your sturdy body, your tender face will always remain with us. We will change our sorrow into power and follow without deviation the direction you have shown us, until the whole world accepts Communism." Assembly was over. We were worn out by grief.

When I went home, I announced the grievous news that my grandmother already knew. I was surprised that her eyes were not red at all. When she asked me why I had been crying, I told her that I had done as everyone else did. My grandma seemed outraged, but she controlled herself. I heard her muttering, "Mao, you who always spoke of the soul in your speeches, take care of your own . . . ." Then she held out some books to me that she had found in a trash can. "Here, Niu-Niu! All these books are extraordinary. They'll help you cultivate your heart, your soul and your mind. Read them, my dear. I know you'll find things in them that will interest you, but hide them well. You know it's forbidden to read anything but Mao's books."

I took the books and sat on the bed to calm down, but it didn't work. My eyes resting on the characters brought up other images. Who was I then? My grandmother's darling? The daughter of my parents? Or else one of Mao's good children? Or had I come into the world to steal and live like a dog?

Several months after Mao's death, firecrackers and the banging of gongs sounded in the streets. People were dancing, gathering in little groups to talk, while others happily pasted new propaganda posters over the old ones. I followed the crowd toward the square to find out what was going on. Smiles had reappeared on people's faces and relief could be seen in people's eyes. The jubilant population banged on tin pots to make the most noise possible. Some carried placards saying, *Down with the Gang of Four! They are dethroned! The Cultural Revolution is over!*

No one took the time to explain to me what this gang was. They just continued to shout, "Down with Jiang Qing! Down with Chang, Ch'uan Ch'iao . . . ." I knew that Jiang Qing was Mao's widow. How did they dare drag her name in the mud? And then they had always told us that it was necessary to continue the Revolution to the end. How come it was finished then? Things were not that good . . . . Here were these reckless people who were not afraid of dying.

These events also baffled my grandmother. As far as she was concerned, they had discovered four new criminals and, as always, the population rejoiced in it. That was all.

In the weeks that followed, I learned that it was because of these four people in question that we had been subjected to ten years of the Cultural Revolution. Street rumors inflated the number of people liberated beyond the two hundred thousand already announced in the newspaper, *The Red Flag.* For five hours, my grandmother had been listening intently to the loudspeakers; for the last two she kept shaking her head. She pointed toward the loudspeaker. "Niu-Niu, did you hear that? How can this be true? The Revolution is at an end, really ended . . . . My God, everything is going to change!"

She couldn't stay still. These five hours had changed her, as she called upon her absent son. "Did you hear that? Did you see? Everything is going to change. It's finished! Finally the years of suffering are over." She swept me into her arms and wept silently. When she was at the end of her strength she let go of me, reaching under the bed where she searched and found yellowed black-and-white snapshots.

"My son, the day has finally come. Are you still alive? Quickly come back to me. Let your mother get a look at you and put her arms around you. You know how terribly I've missed you these last years? Let me look at you one more time, even if I have to die right after that. That way I can return Niu-Niu to you. My son, do you hear what your mother is saying?"

After weeks of popular festivities and meetings criticizing the Gang of Four, things had really changed a great deal. Grandmother Lei could now come openly to our house in broad daylight. At school a new teacher graded my work and I did well.

Chou Chiang hadn't been to school in a whole week. I went to his house, but the door was closed and two strips of tape had been placed crisscross over it to indicate that entry was forbidden. On the walls of his house, propaganda posters were pasted one over the other. I could make out some of the words: *Chou Pinghua, the criminal, has finally been unmasked by the people.*

I couldn't believe my eyes. I had difficulty reading it. Who would allow himself to criticize the neighborhood boss? Had he fallen at the same time as the Gang of Four? For a week I kept returning to the abandoned house in hopes of encountering Chou Chiang, but in vain.

One day at the end of class, I finally saw him, leaning against our tree. "Chou Chiang, I've missed you so much! Why weren't you at school?"

He didn't smile as I had hoped, but kept his head bowed without saying a word.

"Chou Chiang, what's happened? You can tell me . . . . You know that all your friends in class are thinking of you."

In an almost inaudible whisper he said, "I've been here since the beginning of the afternoon just to see you."

When he lifted his head, I could see that my handsome Chou Chiang's expression was one of overwhelming distress. "Niu-Niu, you still want to be my friend? You still like me?"

"Of course. For a whole week I've been going over to your house to see you."

He finally admitted that his parents were in prison, having been told that they were criminals and killers who no longer had the right to live in their house. Now Chou Chiang lived with his father's sister. My Prince Charming, my adorable Chou Chiang, was undergoing the same reversal of fortune I had lived through. We were sitting at the foot of the tree. He was weeping and I didn't know what to do to comfort him. The liquidation of the Cultural Revolution demanded a new crop of culprits.

"Niu-Niu, my aunt told me that my parents would spend a long time in prison. I know you don't like them . . . but I miss them so much."

I understood very well. I wished that he would cheer up, so I swore to him that I would never leave him. "Chou Chiang, you know I would like to marry you. Don't be sad about your parents. I'll come cook for you and clean your clothes. I won't leave you even if you beat me."

"But now I won't have any more goodies to give you!"

"We can collect paper the way my grandmother does."

He asked me to teach him how, which I proudly promised to do. We remained next to each other under our tree until he felt reassured, until he realized that he still had a friend. Only then did I return home.

I asked my grandmother for permission to marry Chou Chiang. She burst out laughing, saying it was still a little too soon for that. The similarity of our misfortunes had brought us close again. He often came to the house and my grandmother forgot who his father had been. She was every bit as nice to him as she was to me. When she bought something good, we always shared amongst the three of us. Together we made matchboxes, while my grandma taught us poems. Little by little, Chou Chiang adjusted to his miserable new existence. I introduced him to my friends, Ta-Chün, Chin Yen and the others, who greeted him with open arms.

A year went by. I was a little over eleven years old. Hua Quo-feng was in power. People allowed themselves to express their grievances on *ta tsu paos* (as wall posters were known). It was risky. Chin Yen, dressed with a certain elegance, came to inform me of the liberation of her father, who, upon leaving the "stable," had received his back pay. The Housing Bureau had put up the family in an apartment. She invited me to visit.

"Niu-Niu, how do you like my new clothes?"

I was green with envy. I would have given a lot to see my parents too. I was sick of waiting. That's why I refused Chin Yen's invitation, because I couldn't face a happily reunited family.

Tien Yeh's mother had returned from the country and they too were settled in an apartment. She had bought clothes, food and art supplies. When he invited me, I accepted his invitation. Their apartment was spacious, nicely decorated and a pleasant place to live. His mother offered me lots of bonbons. Tien Yeh had asked me if I knew when my own parents would return. Returning to our shack, I raised questions that I had not dared ask for an eternity. "Grandma, do you know when my parents are coming back? And where is my sister?"

From that time on, day and night we waited for their return. In vain we scanned the street from our doorstep looking for familiar faces. When we were in bed and heard footsteps, my grandmother would call out their names and I would join in, anxiously calling, "Mama! Papa!"

We had saved some of our flour for the day of their return. Since there were fewer posters now, my grandmother had less to collect from the trash cans, and we were poorer. Nevertheless, we tried to put aside as many good things as possible in anticipation of the hypothetical arrival of my parents.

The Cultural Revolution had been over for two years, but my parents had not come back. My grandmother talked to herself, wiping her eyes before the yellowed photo, while I dreamed of throwing myself into the arms of those who were gradually becoming phantoms. Little by little, our futile waiting had dampened our hopes.

In the arms of her grandmother

Niu-Niu at age 1 1/2

With Professor Yang

At age 2 with her family

With her little sister Ling-Ling

Dressed like a Hong Kong girl
in a forbidden hotel

Her school, which had been an ancient temple

With Yann and her parents on her wedding day

 Chapter 16

THE RETURN

One Sunday in the spring of 1978, I was sitting on the wooden doorstep enjoying the weather. The sun was high in the sky and the perfume of the trees and the flowers seemed to intoxicate the birds singing from the electric lines. The enchanted atmosphere reminded me of a poem by Li Po which lulled me with its voluptuous, yet simple, lines. To take advantage of a day when I was in such a good mood, I had gone to gather wild flowers. When I got back to the house at about four in the afternoon, I sat on the doorstep to arrange my bouquet, all the while nibbling on a sweet potato that my grandma had cooked for me.

Suddenly some strangers appeared, staring at me. They were even more shabbily dressed than I was. I was overwhelmed by the man's odor; his head was shaved and he held a shopping bag. The other, wearing a hat, was carrying a runny-nosed filthy child. The three of them just stood there, staring at me. They looked like beggars; I coldly informed them we had nothing to give. Then I went back to my bouquet.

They continued to stand there staring at me strangely, and peering into our shack. The man with the hat asked me in a worried voice, "Isn't your name Niu-Niu?"

I was aghast that they knew my name; I shook my head in denial. The other one stepped forward, crouching down to examine me. I became really frightened and called my grand-mother for help. She came running and I pointed to these two alien creatures. "They're scaring me!"

My grandmother asked them pleasantly what they wanted. They remained silent and looked at her with the same unsettling stare.

"If you want some food, I have only one or two sweet potatoes to offer you."

My grandmother was going to get them when she suddenly turned around, looking hard at the intruders. They all stared silently at each other. The man with the hat put the child down and quietly came up to Grandma, stammering, "You . . . you don't recognize us any more?"

My grandmother faltered. Her eyes opened wide as she covered her open mouth with her hand. Her face had undergone a complete transformation.

"Is it true? Is it you? You're still alive?"

"Yes, it's us, your children . . . Mother. And you're still alive too!"

"My children! My son!"

All three threw themselves into each other's arms, weeping, stammering. The dirty little child pulled the man's sleeve and called him "Mama," which I found rather comical. Since the excited adults weren't paying any attention to her, she turned to me or maybe she was attracted by the sweet potato that I was holding. She was drooling in a way that I found very unattractive and rude.

Nevertheless, her funny and likeable look — she was wearing heavy quilted winter clothes even though the weather was warm and her ponytail resembled a New Year's firecracker — charmed me into giving her my delicious potato. She was so hungry that she grabbed it from me without saying "thank you" and swallowed it down in one gulp. Then she wiped her mouth with the back of her hand and gave me a coquettish smile. She looked at my flowers with such eagerness that I couldn't resist giving her some of them. Seeming satisfied, she went back to the man in the hat. "Mama, look at the flowers, they're mine. They're pretty, aren't they?" Her accent was so marked that I had trouble understanding her.

At last the others had wept their fill and Grandma asked them inside. I watched these strangers warily as I stood behind her, using her as a shield. Suddenly remembering that I was there too, she called out, "Niu-Niu, it's them! These are your parents! The ones you've waited for so long!" And she pushed me toward the man, telling me to call him "Mama."

This man came forward slowly, with caution and fear, as if I were some treasure. He caressed my head, my hair, my face, repeating, "I've missed you terribly, my child. There hasn't been a day in these eight years that I haven't thought of you." In spite of the tenderness of these words, I couldn't imagine that this person could be my mother. She was wearing a very masculine hat and when she took me in her thin arms, her protruding bones hurt me. I ran back behind Grandma.

I tried as hard as I could to find the slightest resemblance in these two to the picture of my parents that I had remembered, but nothing seemed to fit. They tried nonetheless to convince me. "Niu-Niu, it's us! Your parents! We used to take you to the park when you were little!"

I really had such a longing for my parents that I wanted to call them Mama and Papa. I had thought of them every day, rehearsing our reunion, but now I could only murmur an awkward, "Hello, gentlemen."

That upset them, but my grandmother tried to explain to them that I wasn't used to them yet, and that they should give me time.

That evening my grandma spent all our money to buy a bit of pork fat and with the flour that she had parsimoniously saved, she prepared a large bowl of noodles. During the meal each of them seemed about to speak, but then stopped and remained silent. The table was drowned in the adults' tears, while the little girl steadily examined me with her large, inquisitive eyes. "Mama told me I had two sisters. Which one are you?"

I didn't know how to answer and to change the subject, I asked her what her own name was. "My name is Ling Ling. I'm already almost eight."

She was adorable. I had just discovered my little sister. I fell in love with her then and there.

That night we were all crowded into the one bed, so warm, so sweet. I was awakened from deep sleep by a conversation between my grandmother and my parents. They were telling her what had happened from the day that the truck took them away.

The Red Guard had done everything to make them confess to crimes they hadn't committed. Then they locked them up in separate cells.

"I would never have believed that Ling Ling would be born and thrive."

After four years of incarceration, they were taken along with other intellectuals into the countryside of another province. They had mailed us many letters that never arrived. They hadn't known if we were still alive. Two years before, they had heard that the Revolution was over and was now condemned by the government. Full of hope, they had put in a request for rehabilitation to the village chief, but they continued to be treated as criminals.

They had become very discouraged until, a week ago, they

were called to the village mayor's office. They were told that their problems had been resolved, that they could return home provided they never spoke about what had happened to them. As soon as they arrived in Chengdu, they went to our old house, but no one could tell them where we were living. It was only in the late afternoon that they found out. Until the day before, they had serious doubts that they would ever see us again.

My grandmother told them how much I had suffered; she did not mention her own suffering. She gave them a glossed-over version of my grandfather's death. Remaining under the covers until early morning, I listened as though hearing the final act of this drama from behind the scenes.

When it was time for me to get ready for school, my mother fixed my hair and my father brought me my breakfast. For the first time in my life, both my parents took me by the hand to take me to school. Because they had returned, I was no longer the wild child, but walked solemnly, my head held high, between the two pillars of my regained pride. I really savored these intense moments. Before they disappeared, as the door of my classroom closed behind me, I turned around to take another good look. I wanted to call them "Mama" and "Papa," but I still couldn't bring myself to do it. That day I could not concentrate on my schoolwork. I was obsessed by my parents' faces; why had it taken them so long to come back to me?

Two days later my mother went with Ling Ling and me to the public baths. When I took off my clothes, the sight of my body made my mother literally sick to her stomach. I had grown used to my pus-filled pimples; now I suddenly felt ashamed and angry. I got dressed again and fled without listening when my mother called me back. I hated my ugly, repulsive body. I hated my parents, and blamed them for this.

I hated even more my mother's look of horror and the nausea that I had caused her.

I had tried to get closer to my parents, but everything had fallen apart. I told myself that this stranger of a mother detested me and all I wanted to do was to throw myself into the loving arms of my grandma who worshipped me.

"I don't love these two people," I said to her. "I hate them."

"Who are you talking about?"

"My parents! These two people that I don't even know!"

Eight years alone with my grandmother had dulled the natural need for my parents. In the days that followed I let them approach me, but behaved coldly toward them. Finally, I had to face the facts: they wanted the best for me. My mother cleaned my clothes by boiling them. My father came to get me from school and sometimes gave me a candy. I noticed that they were also very considerate to Grandma and Ling Ling. They encouraged my grandmother to rest and generally tried to make a better life for all five of us.

It wasn't long before Mimi joined us. My parents had written to the woman she was staying with, asking her to let my big sister return. I had thought about Mimi a great deal. She had left me her little pen and asked me to visit her, but very shortly after her departure, my grandmother stopped writing to her in order not to get her into trouble.

There was pandemonium at the station on the day of Mimi's arrival; crowds were everywhere. At last the train appeared in a cloud of steam, pulling up alongside the platform. But Mimi was not on this train. We waited another four hours in the midst of a noisy, shouting, shoving human swarm until the second train finally arrived. But once again we were disappointed; we couldn't find Mimi anywhere. We were moving despondently toward the exit when we ran into two young peasant girls.

My mother stopped in front of one of them as if struck by a thunderbolt. "That's Mimi! I feel that it's Mimi!"

After a moment we fell into each other's arms. At long last, all of us, except Grandpa, were reunited. It was a kind of miracle!

Mimi had changed. Her hair was very long and her skin had darkened in the country sun. I knew that she was only eighteen years old, but she looked like an adult. No doubt, she too had tasted bitterness. Eight endless years of pain had come to an end and if we spoke of them at all, we played down our saddest memories in order not to tarnish our happy reunion.

Three weeks after my parents returned, we were allowed to move into an apartment with two rooms and a kitchen, with toilets on the landing. Moving was very easy, since we had no furnishings to speak of — just boards, some pieces of material and a few books. My father made a small bed for Ling Ling and me that took up all the space in the kitchen. My parents' work unit had lent them two beds, one for Mimi and my grandmother, the other for my parents on the second floor. We enjoyed the three rooms where we slept two to a bed. The table, chairs and shelves had also been furnished by the work unit, which owned the building. My parents were expected to pay for the furniture from their next paycheck. The compensation payment that had been made to them for their eight years of prison hardly covered our daily expenses during the first two unhappy months.

I left our old shack with regret. Whether horrible or happy, my childhood had left its mark there. The walls were still plastered with newspapers that kept out the cold, as well as with my endless drawings which had helped me fight despair.

One day my mother took me to see a doctor. I had no desire to take my clothes off to reveal my hateful body, but she said we were going there to take care of that very condition. After examining me, the doctor said that this illness was incurable, explaining coldly that he had no time for explanations. My mother grabbed him by the collar and shouted, "You have no right! You must heal her! You can't leave her like this all her life!"

I hadn't known that my mother could get so angry. I tried to calm her, telling her it wasn't that serious. She let go of the doctor and tearfully declared that she would find someone else at any cost, even if it took all she had. And she did make a tremendous effort to find someone; she was the first to leave the house in the morning and the last to return at night. She finally did find an expert in traditional medicine, not attached to any hospital; an old gentleman whom I later called "Grandpa." He was a good man who knew that we were poor and never took money for the visits.

He began by cleaning my skin. Then he brought out his scalpel to scrape off the infected area until new skin appeared. At his every touch I felt as if someone were cutting my nerves. At last he smeared me with a dark substance and finished by covering me with bandages.

My mother seemed to suffer more than I did. I understood then that she loved me very much. Her hand trembled the day that she herself had to clean my wounds. I suffered like a martyr, but from then on I felt the strength of her love and I did not want to say anything. I pressed my lips together in order not to cry out — and not to make her cry.

"No, I can't, Niu-Niu. I feel as though I'm killing you. Why don't you cry? That would help."

"But you're not hurting me at all, Mama. I don't cry so you won't be upset."

"My God, you called me 'Mama'! I'm not dreaming, am I? You know I've waited such a long time for that word." She threw her arms around me. "I love you, Niu-Niu, you know. I am really sorry for everything you've suffered because of us. Forgive me! I beg you to call me 'Mama' again!"

I was dying to do it, but suddenly, for some reason, I found myself unable to say it. She seemed to understand; she did not insist and continued nursing me. How difficult it was to get used to having a mother. For eight years, Grandma had taken her place in my heart and now I found it hard to be comfortable with my mother.

A month went by. My parents no longer allowed Grandma to collect paper from the trash cans. They taught me and my sisters to treat her with the greatest respect, to avoid worrying her or overworking her. At the table she now got the best portions, since we were all worried about her health.

My parents also took great interest in us children. Mimi, who had done dancing exercises ever since she was six, had continued practicing in the country. Now she took lessons from a professor who was an old friend of my parents. They were also very concerned about Ling Ling's education, as well as my own. The attention they gave us touched me deeply, but their pain touched me as well. I heard my mother weeping behind their bedroom door, asking my father if it was really true that we were all together, that it was really all finished, that they had returned for good. She moaned, repeating that everything frightened her. She kept pitying my grandmother, Mimi and me. She was horrorstruck at all the torments we had gone through. She felt guilty about my grandfather's death and wished that she could pay her respects to his ashes.

I was upset by her sorrow. I didn't want to hurt her anymore, or keep her waiting for my affection. So the following morning when she was comforting me while tending my sores, I threw my arms around her. "Mama, I love you! I've missed you so much! I waited such a long time. I've needed you ever since the day you left. I'm so happy just to be a normal girl with a mother who loves me."

My parents went back to work. Mama woke at dawn to do her gymnastic and vocal exercises. She was preparing to play her first role since her return to the theater. Since the showers were located below our window, we were awakened each morning by her practicing in the shower. My father laughed with pleasure, remarking that this whetted his appetite. Unfortunately, we still didn't have that much to eat. I noticed that they still seemed to love each other very much, although it occured to me that they may have been especially demonstrative in front of us to help bring the family closer together.

My father no longer worked in the theater but in a film studio where he had begun writing a script. He was working on the story of a singer during the Cultural Revolution. It seemed he was no longer afraid of the censor; he was convinced China was turning over a new leaf.

The day that they received their first paycheck, Papa and Mama went out for the whole afternoon to buy gifts that they had planned for us for a long time: a pair of shoes for Ling

Ling, a dress for Mimi, warm clothes for Grandma and a pretty pair of pants for me. They bought themselves nothing, except a pack of cigarettes for my father.

Rehearsals for the play had ended. My mother was to appear in public after an absence of eight years. She was nervous all day, asking us if we thought she would play well, if she would please the audience, if she wasn't too old for the part . . . . Before leaving she couldn't eat a thing.

All of us put on our best clothes and Papa bought each one of us an Eskimo bar. We children were not the only ones to shout with joy, letting everyone know that it was our mother who was performing on stage. My father, too, gathered people together to point out his wife, "the one dressed in blue on the left of the stage." Fortunately, in spite of the racket we all made, the play was a success. Mama was inspired, magnificent! We wept with happiness, as did everyone around us at this proof that the ten empty years of the Cultural Revolution were finally over.

We celebrated our first New Year together. My parents had saved for six months to buy firecrackers, meat, candy and fruit. Ling Ling was put in charge of flouring the table, Mimi and my grandmother rolled out the dough and shaped the dumplings. While the water was heating, I lined them up so they didn't stick together. Delighted to be together, we savored these dumplings, solemnly making New Year's resolutions. Once again we could believe in happiness.

Chapter 17

MY GREATEST HOPES

Our lives had now changed for the better. I was no longer the daughter of criminals, the target of slurs by a vindictive, brainwashed society. I now attended high school, while Ling Ling had entered my old school. My sister Mimi danced every day and my recovery was going well. We had all gained weight and our rounded cheeks were rosy. My parents worked hard. My father was happiest because he had just had his script approved. He said that the Liu family had not been destroyed and he was sure that everything would get better and better.

Several months later, against all expectations and in spite of the fact that as the daughter of ex-criminals she was graded more harshly than others, my older sister passed her exam to enter the university. My parents hesitated to let her leave for Beijing, since she had been reunited with the family for barely a year. But they had to think of her future. She had an extraordinary opportunity in being able to enter the only university in the country specializing in dance. On the eve of her departure, no one but Ling Ling went to bed: we all wanted to spend time with her. My mother and grandmother helped her with her luggage and Papa gave her last-minute advice.

"Don't cry, Mimi. Don't be sad to leave us. Mama and I are prouder of you than you can imagine. All I ask is that you write to us whenever you have time. You know we'll want to

hear about everything you do. But finally ... I don't know where
we'll find the courage to let you go . . ."

Mimi promised to get the best grades to thank our parents for their affection. Mama replied that she should be thanking Mimi. She regretted that they had had so little time to take
care of her. "Your leaving again breaks our hearts. We're
ashamed we can't offer you more clothes and money. Over
there in the North you'll have to lead your own life, you can only
count on yourself. All we can do is pray that you'll be happy and
successful."

Our family now consisted of only five members, but we were
still poor. Out of my parents' salary of a hundred and twenty
yuans they sent thirty-five yuans each month to Mimi; Mama
explained she had to eat well to keep her strength up. And
a twenty-year-old girl had to look presentable when she
went out. So the eighty-five yuans left for the five of us had
to go for food, my medication, the rent for the apartment,
electricity and school expenses. Despite my mother's efforts
to make ends meet, we were always penniless by the end of the
month. Grandma suggested that she should make matchboxes
again, an idea which my parents immediately rejected; they
refused to let her kill herself with work.

To ease the food budget, all weekend long we ate a soup
my mother made from pork feet and soybeans. She purchased only the cheapest fruit in season. One day she acquired a
pound of expensive cherries, which Ling Ling and I were to
share and which she put in a cupboard that my father had
installed on the landing. When I went to take some, I found
to my amazement there were only three left in the bowl — one
as tiny as a pea, the second rotten and the third green. My little sister had gulped down my share. She had the tiresome
habit of claiming — or grabbing — more than anyone else. But

Ling Ling was so adorable and so much fun that I could never hold a grudge against her.

One night we were awakened by the sound of our parents arguing. My father demanded some change from my mother, who held the purse strings. He wanted to buy a pack of cigarettes, complaining he never had any pocket money.

"It's not that I don't want to give you any," my mother said, "it's just that we don't have enough! Not even enough to buy a third pair of underwear for each of us."

My father didn't want to listen and they continued arguing. Suddenly there came the sound of a slap from behind the door and Ling Ling and I, frightened, dashed into their room. Papa, regretting his outburst of violence, apologized and swore never to do that again.

"No, don't apologize. It's my fault. I should have bought you some cigarettes."

The next day I noticed that my grandmother had surreptitiously begun again the laborious work of making matchboxes to help out at the end of the month. I helped her as before and we were able to buy extra food which we discreetly added to the household larder.

It was only when my father began shooting his film and my mother had more acting engagements that our standard of living rose above the poverty level. We succeeded in saving five yuans each month and in having meat two or three times a week. From time to time we went to the park to amuse ourselves taking photographs. And the news that Mimi sent us added to our modest pleasures.

Good news would soon come to surprise the family. Our old house, where my parents had been married and Mimi and I were born, was restored to us by the government. In addition, we were awarded damages of two thousand yuans.

It was enough to make my grandma smile to herself for hours, only to turn abruptly thoughtful. For some time I had noticed that she was growing more frail. It had begun with my parents' return, but it was really the result of those difficult years which had exhausted and drained her. Having completed her job, she no doubt now thought herself entitled to leave. Like my grandpa in his time, she often spoke of death and leaving. We worried about her, trying to make her happy. My parents left the two thousand yuans at her disposal, but she spent only fifty to buy an astronomical quantity of white cloth. None of us understood why she wanted it until she explained to us that she was afraid it was cold and dark "up there" and that Grandpa surely needed it.

It was three or four months after the house had been returned to us before Grandma dared to go and look at it. The house had been greatly neglected. Eight years of wind and rain had turned the door brown. The walls were moldy and dilapidated; the garden and the court had lost their flowers. Everywhere the ground was strewn with debris. As her memories flooded back, my grandmother examined every square inch. "Time passes so fast. All this is just an old story now."

Her eyes were red, while I didn't know whether to be sad or happy to see this place again. She told me that during these sordid years she had often had the desire to go and look at this bit of the past. "But I didn't dare set foot on this street . . . . I felt so terrible . . . ."

She was not wrong, for my parents had gone only once or twice and had come back looking sad. Two families of tenants had been living in the house and because they couldn't find another apartment, they had no place to move. Grandma couldn't bring herself to evict them, and asked for a very low rent. One day, nonetheless, she took it into her head to ask my parents to let her live alone in the empty room which had been the living room. "Perhaps he'll come looking for me there."

My parents did not consent to this mad whim. We constantly had to watch Grandma's health and to distract her from gloomy memories. So she satisfied herself by returning regularly to the old house to clean the court and plant flowers in the garden. The frequency of these visits increased and so did their duration. No one suspected what she was doing until the day I heard my mother telling my father that Grandma had redone the living room exactly as it had been before, except for different wall covering. Grandma's obsession with death had by now become habitual, creating among us all a disturbing sense of guilt.

Loneliness had always been a problem of mine and I was still afraid of making new acquaintances. I had my friend Chou Chiang, but even though no one insulted me any more, I did not make new friends. I was so much in the habit of feeling self-conscious I couldn't rid myself of it, so I confined myself to seeing old friends who were also adjusting to life after the Revolution. Our friendship was firmer than ever as we continued to hold to our oath of eternal fidelity.

As a result of a petty squabble with the most violent girl in the school, I was beaten up without fighting back. I was always afraid of the teachers' criticism sessions and I bore in mind my grandmother's wise admonition that one should resign oneself to the blows. But my father didn't feel that way when he saw me returning to the house with my swollen face and cut hands.

"Niu-Niu, from now on you are not going to be a victim. If someone hits you, you hit back! And if you can't hit hard enough, you can bite or pinch to fight back anyway you can. If you lose, keep your dignity and don't cry. If you win, Papa will give you candy."

My mother and grandmother were alarmed to hear him inciting me to fight, but he was furious at the idea that I was still being harassed. In addition, he had decided to go to the school himself to make it clear that if anyone touched a hair of my head again, he would show them who they were dealing with. Thus I had to navigate between my father's belligerence and my mother's passivity. I had to admit that my father's words pleased me more. He took me aside to add, "You mustn't be afraid of the others. They have no right to humiliate you. You have to prove to them you are more intelligent and stronger than they are. I have confidence in you. You'll win all the fights."

From that day on, I fought like a rooster, impelled by the desire for revenge and sure that I was now like everyone else. No one had the right to drag me through the mud any more or treat me like the runt of the litter. I was all too inclined to follow my father's advice and he learned to regret it. I fought once a day as naturally as I ate my meals. If no one bothered me, I fought to help out my friends. The sound of a fight excited me like a drug and I was eager to join in; I didn't worry about who was involved. My reputation at school grew day by day.

One day when Chou Chiang and I were hanging on the parallel bars, some little brat threw a rock, hitting Chou Chiang in the face. It hurt so much that he fell back, crying. Ever since the disgrace and banishment of his parents, Chou Chiang had become as passive and vulnerable as I had been for eight years. Sure of my new strength and not about to allow anyone to take advantage of another's weakness, I shouted insults at the kid. He punched me hard in the face and, seeing stars, I collapsed on the ground.

"If I don't hit you till you mess your pants, my name's not Niu-Niu!"

Chou Chiang didn't know what to do; he shouted at me to stop, but I had an invincible will to prove at last who I was. We fought furiously. My strength rose in me like sap in a tree. I was the victor, leaving my opponent with a bloody nose and half his teeth broken.

The next afternoon my father was called to the high school by the teachers. They told him that he had failed at raising me, that he had to pay attention to my attitude. Contrary to my expectations he didn't lecture me; he actually congratulated me on my courage and firmness. But, he added, he didn't think it was necessary to break the enemy's teeth.

My mother blazed up like a flame. "You're both equally stupid. Three days ago, your father fought with a worker. Your father's head is still bandaged and now today you're going at it too. Really now, is everybody in this family irresponsible? I'm going to tell Grandma everything."

My father became nervous, for of all the members of his family, he was afraid only of his mother. So because of my own misadventure, I found out why my father's head was bandaged. Less amusing was the fact that my parents had to pay the dental expenses of the boy I had beaten.

At the high school we no longer studied Mao's maxims, but the lessons bored me just as much; I often played hooky or surreptitiously read my parents' novels or my dad's scripts in class. In the evening, instead of doing my homework, I would sneak into the line in front of the movie houses and theaters with my little sister and my friends and get in without paying.

My parents began to express some reservations about what had been their unconditional love for their dear daughter. They were distressed that I was so unruly and irresponsible. Before a new dispute broke out, I asked my grandmother to convince my parents that it was better for me to read worthwhile books than to sit in on boring high school courses.

My parents also worried about my relationship with my old friends, who were as aggressive as I was and who did not respect the separation of the sexes expected of people our age. Once we had been known as children of criminals; now we were called "little hoodlums." And as in the past, we got together to steal, break windows and then celebrate by partying in a restaurant. The result was that my father became known for his films and I became famous for my misdeeds. People knew that the second daughter of the great film director was called Niu-Niu and that she cut classes in order to amuse herself with boys her own age.

There was one good grade on my report card — for having done an excellent job cleaning the classroom. The rest formed a magnificent garland of zeros. At last I noted with a jaundiced eye that vacation time was coming and that my sister would be returning from Beijing. She was going to have praise and gifts heaped on her by the whole family. I was jealous of the love she seemed to inspire in others. She really had to be amazingly lucky! My parents spoke of her as a model to me, which I found very exasperating; she was beautiful, intelligent, and so forth. On the other hand, my mother thought that my own future did not look too promising. She would have been quite satisfied if any of my teachers had anything good at all to say about me.

This injustice, this pessimism about me, this belittling of my abilities made me want to show them that the second daughter of the family could also accomplish great things. What's more, I felt that I had lost my parents' love, a thing I found intolerable.

I buckled down to work, determined to cram my head with information about subjects that repelled me, but which was easy to learn. My next set of grades shot up, which led my parents to assume that I had cheated. This new insult was even harder to take than the earlier ones and I suggested they check my grades with my professors.

I wrote an essay that has since become part of family history. Its title was "My Greatest Hopes." I wrote it because it was the truth.

> Ever since I was young, I have had a number of 'great hopes.' I always wanted to make my family proud of me, so that everyone would be kind to me and love me for what I am. I hope that when I am an adult, I can accomplish worthwhile things, even if I don't know yet how to begin. But I certainly have a desire to succeed one day and to receive red roses and applause in recognition of what *I* have done. I'd like to be someone different, who rises above the crowd. I would like to become some great invincible eagle, spreading its wings high in the sky across mountains and clouds . . .

My father was thrilled by this. He hadn't dreamt that I had such heartfelt ambitions. His admiration did my heart good; it gave me the motivation to continue in my own way. I swore to him that as long as I could do what I liked, I wanted above all to make him proud of me. I told him that eight years without him had disoriented my life and destroyed my self-confidence, but that his return had opened up the possibility that I could accomplish something. Papa added that to become a powerful eagle, I had to get serious about my studies. His sincerity convinced me that my parents really loved me.

One result of my essay was the decision that I should go to high school in Chongqing, where I would live with an uncle. Mama reluctantly agreed to let me leave. My father took a week off to go with me to see me settled in this unknown city. Mama kept urging me to study and to read . . . and to burn paper money at her parents' tomb, asking them to pardon her for having neglected their final resting place for so many years. I was supposed to let my parents know as soon as I had done that.

This was the first time since they had come back that I left my parents.

Chapter 18
A DEAD SOUL

Chongqing was a pretty little city right above the Blue River, nestled at the base of mountains shrouded by clouds. Each morning the inhabitants woke to the sound of fog-horns. In the evening, the lights reflected in the water merged with those of the city itself to unite with the stars in the sky.

It was here that my family had lived, generation after generation, here that my grandfather had married my grandmother, here that my father had spent his carefree youth. Each time I walked the streets, I imagined my grandpa striding before me and when I heard vendors' cries, I thought that Grandma had heard the very same sounds. The setting of our family's history that she had described to me was right here before my wondering eyes.

The uncle and aunt who took me in lived a very quiet life. My aunt taught English and my uncle Chinese and history. They had four children, two of whom, both girls, lived at home. Another daughter and a son remained in the countryside; they had not been able to return since the end of the Cultural Revolution. I had seen a picture of them, taken when they were very young. One daughter, my cousin Lien-hua, was more beautiful than her sisters. My aunt seemed sad and didn't answer when I asked when Lien-hua was coming back. My cousin finally told me that I shouldn't ask this question, because Lien-hua had died years earlier. No one, however, could tell me exactly what she had died of and I began to find their attitude puzzling.

They were very kind to me. We went to visit my grandparents' former home which had been transformed into a library. My grandfather's bank, which took up two floors of a building, was now a national bank. They often took me to the movies and together we discussed the films that we had seen, something I enjoyed. I loved this family tremendously.

I was enrolled at the high school where my uncle taught. I made many friends there, one of whom, Meimei, was the best student in the class. She was a good influence on me, so that I often came in second or third in tests, which made my parents happy. Through friends visiting the city, they kept sending me goodies that I shared immediately with my new friend.

Meimei lived in a moored sampan on the shore of the Blue River. Her parents were fishermen; during the off-season, they sold produce grown on a small piece of land allocated to them. Since they were illiterate, all their hopes were pinned on Meimei; they were proud of her for being able to read and write, and they hoped that she would be able to enter the university. On Sundays I went fishing and swimming with them. They offered me a fish to give to my uncle — a modest gift to show their gratitude for the attention he had lavished on their daughter in class. The gift was all the more precious because they themselves could afford to eat fish only two or three times a month. They insisted I stay for dinner in spite of their poverty and the simplicity of their meal.

As I got to know Meimei better, I discovered that their family had serious problems: whether it was on shore or on the river itself, there were endless fights among the fishermen. The best mooring berth or the best fishing spot always went to the strongest. Because of ill health, Meimei's father never won these fights, but even so he had succeeded in finding a place, and a good place to fish at that, by promising his daughter's hand to the half-witted son of a local bigwig. The others, who were envious, tormented him by piercing the hull of his boat, regularly tearing his net and doing damage to his small plot of land. Never could I have imagined that on a river that seemed so tranquil there could be such vicious, meanspirited rivalries. But all was not peaceful within the family either.

"There's nothing in the house and still you keep on drinking. Our life is drowning in liquor — you're nothing but a drunk!"

"To hell with you! I work like a dog and I don't even have the right to a little drink! Bitch!"

When she heard this from outside the house, Meimei didn't dare go in. She was ashamed and asked me to come back some other time. I must not hold it against them, she said: poverty wore everyone down to the same level where a penny wasted caused a household scene. Of course, she did not need to explain. I could still remember the day my grandpa had cursed my grandma for the rotten food we were forced to eat.

Despite this I liked her parents, who were so unaffected and kind. I loved to go fishing with them. Everyone sang a song to show that he had a good catch. Their red faces and hands, their spontaneous laughter after they'd been drinking, had definitely brought a new, picturesque element into my life. But good times last only a moment.

One day my uncle received a long letter which he and my aunt read together. After that the whole family was depressed, cursing Lien-hua's fate from morning till night.

"Lien-hua, my poor child, where are you?"

"What a terrible story, my sister!"

"The dogs, the bastards, I'll kill them all!"

Lien-hua was supposed to be dead, so I didn't understand what the letter could have said. Consumed by grief, the family paid less and less attention to me. Soon it was time for me to return to my parents.

Two months later, rummaging through some of my father's letters, I discovered what terrible mystery lay behind the letter my uncle had received. My beautiful cousin, whom I knew only from her picture, was still alive. During the Cultural Revolution, having confidence in Mao, she had followed his admonitions and gone to the countryside to be reeducated by farm work. There, a few months later, she had become acquainted with a young man on her work team and fallen in love with him. She was exempted from agricultural labor so that she could work at the peasants' local radio station which broadcast political messages through loudspeakers. Inevitably, this stirred up jealousy among the other girls, who maligned her relentlessly. As for her, Lien-hua remained blindly in love for three years, until the day when her boyfriend returned to his parents' house to marry the daughter of the chief labor recruiter in order to get himself a job as a factory worker. He wanted to escape the hard farm life. Lien-hua, abandoned, attempted suicide.

She was saved in time by the head of the farm, help that would bring her nothing but new troubles: now she really fell into the jaws of the tiger. This man, a brutish and stupid peasant, had succeeded in becoming farm chairman during the Cultural Revolution. Since Lien-hua's arrival, he had followed her around like a dog. He wanted to marry this beauty; he had never seen anyone like her. But my cousin would rather have died than marry such an ugly, coarse person. In fact, the year when all the young Maoists had arrived in the village, he had done everything to make their lives unbearable just to flaunt his strength and power. The local peasants didn't welcome these "intellectuals" either, since their arrival meant sharing their already meager grain rations with them. The hateful farm chairman had beaten one starving young fellow to death for stealing a chicken and said, "That's good for all of you! Before, you didn't pay any attention to the peasants, but now you know who you're dealing with. From now on I'll see to it that we put things in the proper light so that you make us peasants look good!"

He began to take it out on Lien-hua. He had failed to seduce her, so he plotted revenge. Gagging her with a handkerchief, he raped her, then made her swear not to tell and not to try suicide because she was still of use to him. He bullied her with the threat of humiliating her by forcing her to appear before a self-criticism session with a pair of shoes around her neck. At that time the most humiliating thing you could do to a woman was to tie a pair of old shoes or slippers around her neck, because they signified that she was "damaged goods" in sexual terms.

Lien-hua was undeterred by threats; she knew perfectly well what the law was, and had written to a higher farm official to demand justice. But since the laws were what the most powerful made of them, my cousin was unable to prove her story. Even though the whole village considered her an innocent victim, no one dared oppose the chief. He became even more arrogant and abusive.

He had her stripped and then raped her, this time in front of a group of intimidated peasants. Afterwards, pleased and proud of himself, he left with a smug smile on his face. From that day, my cousin's soul was dead. She was scorned by everyone; all pity and compassion seemed to have vanished from the village. If one of her companions did consider coming to her aid, he would quickly change his mind, fearing he'd never get permission to return to the city. Not only did they keep away from her, they spat in her face, treating her as a whore. She lost her job at the radio station and had a miscarriage; from then on, she became a vegetable. What's more, she had to do the heaviest work all alone.

After the Cultural Revolution ended, her father, my uncle, tried to get in touch with her, writing many letters that were never answered. He had been told she was dead, which he came to accept. Evidently that monster of a chief had intercepted her mail; the letter that my uncle had received when I lived with them was dated 1976 — it had taken two years to reach its destination. It turned out that an enemy of this terrible man had finally sent it on.

After I left Chongqing, my aunt and uncle immediately left for Yunnan province in order to find their poor Lien-hua, by now half-crazed and changed forever. For four months they petitioned the authorities to begin judicial proceedings against the chief. They finally got to court. The judge ruled that there could be no real proof in an incident that had taken place years earlier. There was no way of verifying whether it had been rape or consensual sex. Since what was done was done, the judge suggested marriage to resolve the case. However, the monster who had tortured my cousin didn't want to marry her now; he said that he refused to take such human garbage for a wife. When her parents went back before the judge, he washed his hands of the whole affair, refusing to hear any more about it.

Feeling completely desperate, my uncle realized that his

daughter's life was ruined since no young man would want to marry her; the only solution was to marry her to the man who had defiled her. Lien-hua had reluctantly agreed to this. It was the only way for her to have a home and to expiate her shame, save face and, consequently, lead a normal life. The entire family was on its knees — begging this creature, promising anything that he demanded. My uncle offered to give him his savings, so that they could buy furniture and whatever else was needed to set up a household, but the rapist continued to balk.

That was one reason why my father had received this heartbreaking letter. Since my father, having made a film there, had acquaintances in the area where Lien-hua lived, my uncle asked him for help. I can remember the last lines of the letter: *Come help me, that's all I ask. All my life I've worked so hard teaching the students good Party principles. At my age my only hope is to see Lien-hua settled, to find a place where she can live peacefully. That is also what she wants now. Even though her eyes are dry, inside herself she is weeping. I beg you on bended knees to come to Lien-hua's aid.*

A month later, my father returned from Yunnan, circles under his eyes. "I don't know if I did the right thing or not, but they're finally married. Lien-hua just sits all day, smiling nervously like a madwoman."

My grandmother said that if she had begun smiling, even like a half-wit, it wasn't so bad; the most important thing for a woman was to save her reputation.

My father, with the help of little presents and dinner invitations to local administrators, had succeeded in his delicate mission of persuading them to pressure my cousin's tormentor if he refused to go through with the marriage. Urged on by Papa, the officials had threatened him with prison. After the wedding, he treated Lien-hua like an animal, beating her and insulting her whenever he pleased. She never complained, but accepted his abuse with the fixed smile of an idiot.

I saw my uncle and aunt four months later. They had aged and their faces had lost their usual cheerful expression. "It was we who forced our children to go and be reeducated in the countryside. Time has punished us for our foolishness and rigidity. We are sorry, we hate ourselves for it. The life of our Lien-hua, our most beautiful and most intelligent child, is finished . . . ."

Some months later I finally met my cousin, who had been given a month's vacation on the occasion of her marriage. She had taken advantage of this to visit us, especially to thank my father. She no longer resembled the photograph in which her black hair shone like brilliant ebony and her snow-white skin framed the dark diamonds of her jewel-like eyes. At twenty-seven, she looked older than my mother; her hair was sprinkled with grey and her face was harsh. She had gained weight and lost her figure. Her smile was as my father had described it — foolish and nervous.

Her monstrous husband had come with her, and Lien-hua seemed terrified of him, bringing him water, food, washing his clothes and even handing him toilet paper when he went to the toilet. Every time he cleared his throat, she hurried to ask him what he wanted. He was unbearably full of himself, passing his days in idleness or going to the movies alone. When they left at the end of the week, my parents went to the station with them. They did it only for my cousin's sake, because they knew that otherwise she would have had to carry all the luggage.

I've never seen her again. Her story gave me nightmares. I knew the strength of the prejudices that prevented young men from marrying her after she had been raped; but it was heartbreaking that not one had dared to defy this social curse to offer her a little love and human warmth.

From their birth, beautiful girls have a short-lived star, is the old proverb that my grandmother had taught me. Unfortunately, it's this attitude that is responsible for the lot of all the Lienhuas of China. As for my cousin, she and her husband had a child — who I thought should never have been born.

Chapter 19

CHOU CHIANG DEPARTS

For my fifteenth birthday Mama bought me new clothes and prepared a sumptuous dinner. My parents' salaries had risen and we no longer suffered from hunger. I invited my friends, Chou Chiang, Ta-Chün, Tien Yeh and Chin Yen to my birthday party.

They had changed. Ta-Chün no longer wanted to enlist in the army. He had set up a little business selling movie tickets on the black market. He was also selling large quantities of vegetables to the North where there was a food shortage. He didn't have to pay the fare when he took these vegetable shipments north because he had made arrangements with the railroad employees. He was earning a hundred to two hundred yuans a month, at that time a small fortune for a single person, money which he was saving to buy a restaurant. He was already looking forward to overcharging disagreeable customers and offering free meals to friends and artists. As always, his big plans amused us.

As for Tien Yeh, he had worked so hard that he passed his entrance exams to the Fine Arts university and was leaving for the capital in September. He was quite proud of this success, which gave him a certain cachet with the girls. To raise some money, he pressured Ta-Chün and me to buy one of his paintings. I had squeezed ten yuans from my father for this purchase, but Ta-Chün had to spend more than fifty!

Chin Yen had finished her secondary studies and thanks to the persistence of her parents, or perhaps the many little gifts they had handed out, she had found employment in the same cloth-weaving mill where they worked. At nineteen, she was very happy, because factory work like this was hard to find. She earned only twenty-eight yuans a month to start, but this was more than enough for her. She was no longer Ta-Chün's "wife" as in the old days. We had all outgrown our childish ways.

Since his parents' departure, Chou Chiang had become taciturn and glum. He barely spoke at dinner. His sad expression made him look older. With only one more year of secondary school to go, the two of us would soon face what our friends already confronted — life as adults. Chou Chiang had no specific plans for his future. He would allow himself to be swept up by the river, so to speak, to see if the current pulled him under or buoyed him up. As he said in his sardonic way, "I have nothing to worry about, the Party declares that there will be no unemployment in China. All I risk is to find myself, as they say, 'waiting for a position.'"

I myself wanted to enter the university and, Chou Chiang's pessimism notwithstanding, I hoped that we would go there together.

After the meal, we decided to make a tour of the town without any idea that this brief pleasure would later cause us some serious problems. As we passed the old theater, feeling nostalgic, we entered. Chou Chiang had revealed the secret of the subterranean passage.

In the large empty auditorium, I noticed that our old hideout had a new face. After the Cultural Revolution it had been reopened, painted, decorated with flamboyant red fabric and equipped with many projectors. When we saw that the stage was set for a play, we decided to put on the actors' costumes and hold a private performance of our own. We found the costumes in the wings, where we forced the door open with a kitchen knife. Since there were no watchmen, we turned on the projectors too. In short, our little circus, our "carrying on," lasted well into the night; eventually Ta-Chün, the up-and-coming businessman, said he could get a good price for these well-made costumes. "It won't be long before we all have to separate. Tien Yeh is leaving and maybe Niu-Niu will join him in Beijing. The others need to go on working here. Why don't we have one fantastic last fling before we split?"

Without asking any questions and in complete agreement, we took all the theater accessories, packing them like professionals. We promised ourselves that no one would divulge our secret: Chou Chiang had to keep to himself because of his new social position; Ta-Chün wanted to avoid interrogation by the police whom he saw rather frequently because of his shady dealings; Chin Yen risked losing her job and Tien Yeh would be barred from his university, so the only person left who could take responsibility for the theft was me! I became all puffed up by my own importance. To prove to my friends that I was courageous and faithful, I gladly accepted such an honorable responsibility.

The next night we sought out our old receiver of stolen goods, who, as usual, said nothing, but bought the whole lot for one hundred yuans. Our rules demanded that this money pay for a feast and if anything was left over, we would share it among us. So that is what we did, and after our big celebration, each of us kept fifteen yuans.

We heard that when the actors discovered that their costumes were gone they were forced to cancel the performance and they notified the police of the theft. We were quite proud of our exploit.

Since we lived in a small town, the police made rapid progress in their investigation and a week later, I came home from high school to find my enraged parents with the policeman and the receiver of stolen goods. They had tracked me down. I honored my promise, and told the police that I had done it alone. The fence confirmed it, because he knew our gang's law of silence.

My father took out the bamboo switch and began to beat me. I carried on with horrible cries of pain. Unfortunately, my grandmother was out of the house at the moment, so no one came to my rescue. Even my mother beat me hard, calling me names. By my count, between the two of them I took a hundred and forty lashes. My father said, "You're really a bad girl. We've tried to give you a good education, but you won't obey us. You're so stupid, you could end up in prison!" Mama screamed that I was a disaster for our family. I had never seen my parents so angry. They made me realize what I had done. I begged them to forgive me, to help me stay out of prison. This time I was really scared.

They did try everything possible to keep me from being put behind bars. It was a painful week, because neighbors who had always detested me and people jealous of my parents made life difficult in this situation where we were so vulnerable. They even made false statements about me to the police.

Mama used her connections to move heaven and earth. The police allowed themselves to be swayed on condition that we pay five hundred yuans plus interest. I also had to spend two hours a week in a school for the reeducation of criminals. To get together such a large sum, my parents had to scrape and borrow. They tried to keep all of this from my grandmother, but she heard about it. She blamed herself for not teaching me properly. The lesson was good for me. I was ashamed of impoverishing my parents and making my grandmother feel guilty, as well as losing face among my high school friends. Neighbors no longer spoke a word to me; they forbade their children to have anything to do with me. My nickname, "Bad Girl," had achieved an ominous notoriety.

In the face of this social ostracism, only one person stayed loyal and faithful whatever happened; that was Chou Chiang. He continuously proved that he would never shun me. We two had a destiny fixed by the stars, he said. His only worry about me was my disturbing habit of playing with fire, although he admitted that this was also part of my charm.

As for myself, I began to find his presence by my side indispensable. When I thought of him, I blushed, my heart beating faster. His seductive smile haunted my dreams. He was my brilliant and handsome hero, just like in the movies. This new feeling, of which I was somewhat frightened, sent me to heaven, but also to hell. I became lovesick; I had read about these symptoms in romantic novels. My intuitive, perceptive mother warned me that I mustn't think of fun with other young people, but concentrate on my studies and my future.

I knew very well that it was shameful for a girl of my age to think about a boy. It was considered a scandal for a girl under twenty years old to mix with boys. Even in high school, the teachers separated the two in their classes, making sure that they didn't have too much to do with each other. I remember when the best student in my class had slipped a note into a girls' inkwell, asking her to go out to the movies with him. He was denounced by a classmate and subjected to an assembly of criticism with his parents present. His father slapped him in front of everyone just to shame him. Afterwards he was demoted and was no longer considered the top student of the class.

This story upset me. I didn't know which way to turn with Chou Chiang, whom I vainly tried to banish from my thoughts. He changed too, blushing every time we met. Our conversations, which had been so spontaneous, now foundered in embarrassment.

I became listless, my head felt hot and I cursed the constraint put on the young. Even so, our relationship was frank and honest and for a good reason. We had known each other since childhood and I couldn't see why I should stop seeing him. So I defied convention in continuing this friendship, even though his growing shyness damaged our former closeness. It made me happy just to feel his breath and the warmth of his body.

"The Bad Girl casts her net for the boys," people were saying. There were always nasty people on the street ready to insult us. My mother had become very strict, ordering me to come home directly after school, particularly since the entrance exams to the university were coming up.

To make a long story short, I flunked the exams, which didn't bother me at all. Despite my reputation as a bad girl, my parents did not expect this, since I had recently done so well in school. Furthermore, in our high school, the best in the city, eighty percent of my classmates had been admitted to the best universities and the rest to respectable institutions. *I* had not made it anywhere. Papa and Mama were angry and wouldn't allow me to see Chou Chiang. They locked me into my room to prepare for the following year's examinations.

Poor Chou Chiang called me from beneath my window. We threw each other little notes. In spite of rain and bad weather, he never missed a single romantic vigil under the tree outside my window. Finally, thanks to my little sister's cooperation, I was able to escape into the country with my old friend.

We remained silent in a meadow, not knowing how to make up for the time we had lost. He took my hand, which was trembling and moist. We were very happy to sit next to each other, listening to the wind and the birds, contemplating the green meadow and the little river. He finally broke the silence to ask me if I remembered the day when we had watched the sunset with Professor Yang. "Yes, of course . . . . We were so little then."

And hand in hand, heart to heart, once again we watched the sun sink over the horizon. Just before leaving, he said words that became engraved in my memory: "It is true that I love you, Niu-Niu." I couldn't sleep for a week.

After this, to be on the safe side, we met only late at night when the city was asleep. He would announce his arrival by throwing a pebble against my window. Since I slept on the first floor, I jumped from the window to join him. We returned when the gong sounded an hour later.

This romantic interlude did not last long. One evening, when the family was quietly watching television, Chou Chiang came to our house dressed in a soldier's uniform. He looked frighteningly haggard. While my parents offered him tea and candy, he explained that he was leaving the next day to fight in the war against Vietnam. He considered himself lucky to have been accepted by the army; this would honor his family as it did those of all military men and women. The news tore my heart out. I couldn't believe it.

My grandmother gave him twenty yuans, telling him to take care of his health, and I was given permission to walk him home. As we walked, my heart was so full that I didn't say a word. He too was silent, but kept wiping his eyes. Arriving at his aunt's house, he said in a shaking voice, "Don't cry, Niu-Niu, I'll write. I swear to you that I'll return."

Under the lurid light of the street lamp, we kissed on the cheek to say goodbye. *The greatest sorrow is to say goodbye upon leaving and adieu upon dying.* This adage that my grandmother had taught me gave me a premonition that our separation would be forever. After spending a sleepless night, I got up before dawn to see him off at the station. I couldn't let him leave just like that and, thinking of surprising him, I prepared some hard-boiled eggs, as I had seen my mother do when my father went off on a trip. Before leaving the house, I filched some candy and cakes and ran to the station, arriving out of breath.

Many soldiers and their families, laughing or crying, were saying their goodbyes. Chou Chiang stood all by himself, a large knapsack on his back, looking miserable as he watched others hugging their nearest and dearest. "Why did you come?" he asked.

I held out my sack of provisions, and begged him to promise me that he'd return. It hurt me to see his gratitude shining in his grey eyes. Suddenly he burst into tears, his whole body trembling. "Don't forget me, Niu-Niu. When I get my first pay, I'll buy you the most beautiful present. Even if a bullet hits me in the stomach . . ."

Chou Chiang, my best friend and brother, but also my love, had such a good heart that in spite of the dangers he faced, he was thinking of me. A horn sounded, announcing the train's departure, my ten-thousand "no's" and our ten-thousand embraces notwithstanding. Our hands drew apart as the train began to move; I watched as it dwindled into the distance and vanished. I knew that Chou Chiang would be wiping his eyes, whispering to me to wait for him, reassuring me that he would return.

In the empty station I saw images of our childhood. Our first encounter at school: "Hello, my name is Chou Chiang." And later, when I had to sweep the court, his "I'll never leave you, Niu-Niu." And now, only so recently, he had bashfully declared his innocent love for me and I, like an idiot, had done nothing to prevent him from leaving . . . .

Chapter 20
BLACKMAIL

One month later, my mother's work unit announced that seven positions were open for children of existing personnel, provided they passed an examination. Three of the openings were for actors, two in food services and two in set design. My parents were out of town at the time, working in the provinces, unaware that their colleagues were fighting to get their offspring admitted. Jealousies and old quarrels had surfaced in the form of letters of denunciation, insults and wall posters.

Since I wanted an acting job, my problem was to be accepted by a former student of my mother's for instruction in dramatic art. My mother had always said that Yen Ying was a brilliant and beautiful young woman with a great future in the profession. Her qualities nevertheless had aroused the envy of her peers, who didn't spare their slanderous remarks. My mother told me that Yen Ying had fled Beijing to escape just such defamation. Our family, however, had never credited gossip. As far as we were concerned Yen Ying was a pleasant and sincere young woman.

She received me with open arms, and began, without delay, to teach me to sing, to dance, to perform little sketches. She also gave me background in the history of literature, painting and theater. I was impressed by her immense knowledge.

The day of the exam, I presented a modern text by Lao She,

Clair de Lune. I was overwhelmed by the emotional experience of re-creating on stage the tragic situations — like hunger and illness — that I had lived through as a child. Abruptly, I froze. Even so, Yen Ying thought that I had done superbly, although I didn't get the part. If my parents had not been away I might have done better.

I was not downcast about it, for I had had the chance of getting to know Yen Ying. It was she who inspired me to work hard to be admitted to the university. Thanks to her, I began to improve myself, to work on my writing style and to learn to judge my father's screenplays.

My parents were astonished and delighted at my changed attitude and I was pleased to make them happy. Yet I kept my plans to enter the university to myself, just in case I failed. I didn't want to lose face or to disappoint them. In spite of the exorbitant cost, my parents were willing to pay for the supplementary courses that I planned to take. They tightened their belts to do it; I had put an end to my foolish pranks to show them I appreciated their effort. And they were proud of my friendship with Yen Ying, which they considered a change from the dubious company I had kept in the past.

Initially, my new friend's candor was disconcerting. She talked about herself openly and without false modesty, contrary to my grandmother's precepts that one should hide one's feelings and remain humble. Yen Ying told me that people were jealous of her, not only because she was beautiful and intelligent, but also because she was still celibate at the age of twenty-seven, something considered abnormal. The fact that she had many friends aroused the envy and suspicion of idle people who pried into other people's lives. It's possible that without people like that, the Cultural Revolution would never have lasted for ten years. In others' eyes, Yen Ying was just too lucky; she should have balanced her virtues with a few well-chosen flaws.

She always expected to meet her soulmate, but after the tidal wave of the Cultural Revolution she doubted that such natures had survived. She admitted to me, not altogether seriously, that she would have married someone like my father, if he had been free.

Yen Ying's perceptive and lively teaching made such an impression on me that even today I model myself on her. She gave me the courage and desire to forge ahead towards success, without kowtowing, without giving up in the face of failure, without sparing myself in order to reach my goal. It was thanks to her that I resolved to attempt the entrance exam in the most difficult section of the film school — namely, film production. If I succeeded, not only would my parents admire me, but I would gain recognition from those who had always hated me. I wanted to prove something to myself.

While I was feverishly preparing for the examination, I heard from my parents that Yen Ying found herself in a delicate situation. She loved a young filmmaker, a colleague of my father's. They had originally met in Beijing long ago, but were not able to marry at the time, as he was doing his military service and she was still a student. When they met again, he had been forced into marriage by his parents.

I knew this young man well. Since my earliest days, I had called him "Big Brother Xu." He was lively and goodhearted. Despite his arranged marriage, he loved Yen Ying passionately. After two years of being apart, they went to restaurants or the movies together. Unfortunately, they were spied upon by those who had eyes for such things.

To put an end to his loveless marriage, Xu asked his wife for a divorce. She went to his superior at work, saying terrible things about Yen Ying. Driven by her wounded ego, she declared that there was no reason why she should be the dupe in this situation and the only one to suffer. Rather than leave the two lovebirds in peace, she wanted all three to suffer. As word of this story spread, Yen Ying, who had long been in a precarious situation, lost her good reputation.

When I went to cheer her up, all her strength was gone; she seemed helpless. She knew the judge would not grant Xu his divorce: there was no evidence that his household had ever been disrupted by marital discord so there were no "objective" grounds for divorce. No one empathized when Xu said, "We no longer love each other." His wife had spread rumors that Yen Ying and Xu had slept together. By claiming to be the victim, she had naturally gathered sympathy from anyone willing to listen to her.

The director of their work unit had sent a letter to Yen Ying's parents; he also demanded that they write a self-critical essay, even though their only crime had been to see each other, to love each other platonically. Yen Ying, although liberal and modern-minded, would never have committed adultery. She was exhausted, helpless in the face of injustice. The grim prospects for her future were always on her mind, reducing her to a tragic and vulnerable silence.

On the very evening of their arrival in the city, her parents were guests at our house — a gesture of support for their daughter. In the face of all this gossip, we tried to reinforce their confidence in her. However, the atmosphere at the dinner table was so tense that we barely touched the many delicious dishes.

A month went by during which Yen Ying went through a veritable hell. She no longer wanted to go out, because people stared at her. She wrote pages of self-criticism. She lost a starring role for which she had already begun to rehearse. Her parents made scenes, demanding that she return to Beijing. They preferred that she lose her job rather than be disgraced. She refused, intent at least on staying in the same city as her love.

Xu quarrelled constantly with his wife, and production of his film was cancelled. Finally, under pressure from his wife, he returned to his parents who, in turn, began preaching to him.

Distraught, Yen Ying came to see us. Her parents had threatened to commit suicide unless she found a husband. My parents rushed to dissuade them, while I stayed with Yin Yang. Two hours went by and I was beginning to yawn when I heard hurrying footsteps on the staircase.

It was my father; his face was livid and wet with perspiration. "Yen Ying, come quickly! Your mother — she cut her wrists!"

After a night of anxiety at the hospital, we were told that Yen Ying's mother was out of danger. Yen Ying went into the room to speak to her. I understood from the sound of sobbing behind the door that in order to make her mother happy, Yen Ying was ready to submit to what had always repelled her.

One month later, Yen Ying married an unknown suitor, a chemistry professor at the university. I attended the wedding. Her prime accusers and the director of her work unit were among the many guests.

Chapter 21
THE LETTER

At last, the two grueling weeks of exams were over. After four elimination exams originally taken by sixteen hundred candidates, only three of us remained: two boys and me. At each stage I went to check on the results; seeing my number on the "passed" list made me so euphoric that I lost a couple of pounds. I didn't know how I had succeeded in passing these elimination tests. By the time they were over, I was thin as a rail. Everything, however, was not over. With fear and trembling, I still had to wait for the final verdict, because in the whole country, only one or two students from each province were to be accepted. Among the three of us, there was bound to be a loser and no one could predict who would be eliminated.

Still, I was preoccupied by thoughts of Chou Chiang, who hadn't written one line since he left, although I had written to him and sent him a shirt bought with pocket money from my mother.

I went to visit Yen Ying after the first results were announced. She had changed, her disposition had dulled, her mood was increasingly bitter. When I asked her what married life was like, she answered that hers was like all the others, that was all. Her husband, who was very nice, did the cooking and laundry for her. He had never touched her since the wedding night, when Yen Ying had brandished a pair of scissors under his nose, forbidding him to approach her. Understanding as he was, the unloved husband expected her request for a divorce to come at any time. He made no secret of the fact that he would do anything to make Yen Ying happy. She was well aware that she was hurting him, but she thought that was only fair, since others had made her suffer so much.

As for Xu, he had given all he owned to his wife in return for their sleeping apart — all things considered, a kind of equitable bargain. Some time after my conversation with Yen Ying, I learned that he had been arrested for having had illicit relations with other women. We were fearful of the sentence that he would receive. Yen Ying, however, found the new situation hopeful, for her own husband had now agreed to a divorce. What is more, since criminals had the right to marry, she was ready to live with Xu despite the years of prison that he faced.

Their dedicated love inspired me to act like Yen Ying when it came to my Chou Chiang. I told myself that even if he returned from the war disabled, my devotion to him would not lessen. But, good heavens, why didn't I get an answer to the letter I had sent three weeks ago?

One morning I awoke in a great mood without knowing quite why. I dressed with unusual care which surprised my little sister, Ling Ling, whom I invited to the movies. When we returned home, the building's caretaker handed me a letter that I hoped was from Chou Chiang. I read it eagerly: "Comrade, we are happy to inform you that you have been accepted into the directing class of the cinema department of the University. Please provide your registration forms before September 3." It was signed, "The Party Cell of the university Cinema Department, Beijing." A huge red seal solemnly decorated the bottom of the page.

So I was a member of the rare elect! No, it had to be a hoax. Reading and rereading the letter, I shouted out insults against the malicious joker who was upsetting my peace of mind. Then I handed the letter to my little sister who couldn't believe her eyes either. I burst into tears and stormed into the house, locking myself in my room. There I was, stroking the magnificent, gigantic red seal as if I had gone mad. It was a genuine letter after all, typed on a machine with the seal embossed in the paper. Even the stationery had a special, inimitable texture.

I had been admitted. This meant that from this day forward both my parents and my enemies would have to respect me. No longer could they shame me. I mussed my hair and jumped on the bed, shrieking with joy. My hopes would finally be realized. This was the bright future that would make it possible for me to gain others' confidence, to be loved. I — the villain, the thief! From now on, I had a reason to hold my head high.

I wanted to give my parents a surprise and enlisted my sister Ling Ling's help. I put my letter on top of the newspaper that they were in the habit of reading as soon as they got home. The two of us began to shout from the window, throwing out old papers as though we were strewing flowers, to attract the attention of passersby.

Finally my parents returned — Ling Ling and I greeting them very respectfully with "Hello, dear Papa and Mama." They looked quizzical. My grandmother asked my father to check on what I was plotting, because I had been singing at the top of my lungs all day. He demanded to know if I'd been brawling again and was celebrating some victory. Then I saw him pick up the newspaper and before I had time to answer, his shout filled the house.

At first he thought the administration had made an error, confusing my name with someone else's. For him, the event was as incredible as if it had rained diamonds. As my sister added her two cents worth confirming that I was telling the truth, my parents became annoyed, thinking that we had somehow fooled them by making up the whole thing. I told them that it was the result of my persistence for the entire year and the reason for my wanting to take supplementary courses. I admitted that I had passed the four preliminary exams in secret. Mama cried with joy but Papa remained incredulous. "Niu-Niu, I am happy that you made all this effort, but I am certain that someone else has the same name as yours."

This time I was angry. Really, my father took me for an idiot! If he doubted my abilities, no wonder others found reasons to hate me. I took the letter from his hand, suggesting that he verify it before I left for Beijing the following September.

Actually, my father was going to find out the truth. He got on his bicycle that same evening to go telephone the film department at the university, where he knew someone. When he got back, he was singing like someone inspired. "My darling, you're really fantastic! You're the only candidate admitted in our province and the youngest in the class for film directors."

The next day my parents got up earlier than usual and skipped work to buy me presents. Later Papa stood at the door of his studio to see the members of his work team, even those whom he didn't know, in order to spread the marvelous news. "My second daughter, Niu-Niu, has been accepted at the university in the directing class. Take a good look at this notification: it's the only one in the whole province!"

He was so comical that the whole family was convulsed with

laughter. My mother had a hard time getting him to go home.

At the table he railed against those who had suggested that the letter might be a fake. At last he placed the precious treasure in his desk drawer, which he locked with a key; he was afraid that I might crumple it or lose it accidentally.

The malicious neighbors now greeted me with friendly smiles: these were the very same people who had jeered at me or forbidden their children to play with me. Still they didn't fail to ask who had given the extra little push to get me admitted. I just answered them ironically. "You know, I'm like the blind cat who catches a dead mouse. I read nothing, studied nothing, spent my time fighting with hoodlums . . . ." Then I went on my way, not without feeling that they were getting their comeuppance. By their lights, my success should have gone to their own righteous and well-mannered offspring and not to someone who had lived so wildly. They found this turn of fate really intolerable: it stuck in their craw.

A rumor made the rounds that I had succeeded because my father had made under-the-table payments. I was so mad, I could have broken all the windows in the neighborhood but Mama promptly dissuaded me because she thought, with good reason, that this would merely confirm the backbiters' opinion of me. They would not have hesitated to send letters of denunciation to my university that would have caused me serious problems.

To share my happiness, I told my faithful friends, Yen Ying, Tien Yeh and Ta-Chün of my success. The latter invited us right away to a sumptuous banquet to celebrate. This time, after good food and drink, no one tried to raise hell at the end of the evening as we had done in the past.

I was jubilant, of course, but the thought of Chou Chiang worried me. The whole Vietnamese campaign had lasted only seventeen days and yet there was no news. Before going home, I got on my bicycle to ask his aunt if my dear friend was all right. She looked at me as if I were a ghost. "Chou Chiang? You don't know what happened to him? It was a month and a half ago during a battle, he was . . ."

"What are you saying? Where is he?"

I felt a sort of fog wrap around me as though I were about to pass out. Why were this woman's eyes red-rimmed and what did she go fetch in the other room? She handed me a knapsack, asking me to open it. It was so heavy that I had trouble lifting it. Inside was a soldier's uniform, some books and a piece of paper with Chou Chiang's handwriting: *Hello, Niu-Niu, I hope that all goes well. I miss you very much, you know* . . . The letter had remained unfinished, but on another sheet of paper were a few lines typed on a machine. *Dear parents: With regret we have to announce to you that your son, a good child of the Party, a good soldier of the people, Comrade Chou Chiang, has left us for a long time. This knapsack belonged to him. Please accept the three hundred yuans that the Army awards as compensation to thank Chou Chiang for his courage and valiant service in the war.*

I felt faint. This was impossible. Chou Chiang could not die, he had promised to return to me, his arms filled with presents. This pack and the sordid three hundred yuans turned my stomach. Was he worth so little? I also wanted to know why his aunt had not gone with him to the station the day he left. He seemed so alone, so bereft of affection. I no longer remember her answer. I only know that I left her wiping her eyes. I even left the bicycle behind, returning on foot, clutching the unfinished letter to my breast.

In the course of the days that followed, I went back to all the places where we had met in the past: school, the theater, the little tree by my window, the meadows outside town where he had told me for the first time that he loved me. Everywhere I sought his face, but nowhere did I find it. Alone in my room, I hit my head against the wall until blood flowed, until I collapsed completely.

When I woke, a doctor dressed in white was at my bedside. The idiot explained that after the tension of the examinations, my sort of condition was only normal. Then I asked that everyone leave the hospital room except my grandmother. "Chou Chiang is gone. He's left me too. Why is it that all the people I love always leave like that?" She didn't answer, and simply held my feverish hands as she gazed at me. I was in the hospital for a week, my head covered in bandages.

To exorcise the deep unhappiness that possessed me, I wrote a poem to Chou Chiang.

> My love, my brother, I embrace you on this white paper.
> Tired, thirsty and stupefied,
> I keep saying goodbye.
> I can't forget your face.
>
> Under the yellow earth you lie alone.
> Nothing is there. Yet yesterday
> You rode on a cloud.
> Your body's tomb is the tomb of my soul.
>
> Again and again I call to you: come back!
> My tears flow into a river of blood
> Whose course I mean to follow.
> Buried memories, love torn away,
> Where is your promise?
> Come back, Chou Chiang, come back.
>
> Cross the mountains and the river:
> I am before you,
> But you, you make no move.

Is your grave filled with flowers
Or is the ground bare?
My love, my brother, I embrace you on this white paper.

To please me, my parents suggested trying to publish my poem in a literary journal, but official Communist morality precluded the circulation of such a pessimistic poem. So I sent thirty copies of my goodbye to strange addresses like "the Moon," "the Sun," "the Theater," "the River," "Paradise," and other destinations created by my delirious imagination. I chose the most beautiful stamps and ran to post them in different mailboxes throughout the city. I was convinced that Chou Chiang would receive them.

Chapter 22

STUDENT LIFE

The day of my departure was approaching. For me it was momentous: it represented the end of my childhood. I was going to live on my own, become an adult. I took three suitcases full of books — some of them my grandmother had found in the trash when I was five years old. I took my down quilt and bandages for my skin condition. I also took along hundreds of admonitions from my parents. At the station, I said goodbye for the last time to them, my grandmother and Ling Ling. I took leave of all the avenues and little streets before departing for Beijing full of uncertainties and dreams.

The university was located in the middle of fields just east of the city. On the bus trip I had been impressed by the cars, the large buildings and Tiananmen Square, which I had seen only in newsreels. Arriving on campus, I was astounded to see large streamers welcoming the new students and to hear music blaring from loudspeakers. My suitcases were carried into the dormitory by friendly fellow students who were already settled in. The place was beautiful, filled with smiling faces and the atmosphere was delightful.

My dormitory room on the third floor was about sixteen feet by thirteen, containing four bunk beds, stacked two by two. I thought how proud each of the new students must be feeling. While I was catching my breath, a girl approached me.

"My name is Kao Lan. You're Niu-Niu and you come from Szechuan Province, if I'm not mistaken . . . ."

She put down what she was holding to help me unpack and make my bed. Then she made a detailed list of the campus's assets: the restaurant, the classrooms, the communal showers . . . . She was so nice that I didn't feel like a stranger. She wasn't tall, but she had a pleasing girlish figure. Seeing her, I felt thin and ugly, but in spite of a small twinge of jealousy, I wanted to make friends with her.

Three more roommates arrived in the late afternoon who, just as enthralled as I had been, did not even feel tired from their journey, even though one had come all the way from Tibet. We were all bubbling with excitement and asked each other a thousand questions before leaving happily to take our showers.

The next morning we attended a general meeting, where I saw the rest of the students of my class — fourteen in all, seven girls and seven boys, everyone very shy and dressed alike. Even so, all smiled and warmly shook hands. A professor made the introductions: four of the group with northern accents came from Beijing, while the others, like me, came from provinces farther away. Some had worked in the theater, the movies or in factories. Some had never had professional experience, while others had held many menial jobs here and there. All had made a fantastic effort to obtain admission to the university and had given up their jobs to come here. Their ages ranged from seventeen to thirty-one.

One young man told me that his name was Wu Yen. He was from Beijing and was the oldest of us. To make a living, he had picked up Eskimo bar wrappers in the street. He had a callous and overbearing attitude and was unwilling to admit that a girl of seventeen like me could have the ambition to become a film director. He was not handsome, and his age did not give him any particular status. I didn't find him at all likeable.

On the other hand, Hsiao Ch'uan, another student from Beijing and the youngest of the boys, had a charm that did attract me. He bore some resemblance to Chou Chiang, except that he was taller and more good-looking. He promised to show me his city.

For that same evening, all the students of our section had organized an artistic celebration. There were over a hundred of us. The freshmen wisely stayed on the sidelines, while the others, more at ease, danced to disco. Hsiao Ch'uan came to sit down next to me and talk. He told me that after high school, he had found a job as a stage actor, and that his father was a well-known director — I had, in fact, seen three of his films. His mother headed the capital's largest theater. Nonetheless, he was sympathetic, and not arrogant at all, while his resemblance to Chou Chiang made me feel I had always known him.

A week later courses began. We took eight of them: art history, the history of literature, film history, thesis writing, dramatic art, politics, the history of Communism, and English. I immediately began to study seriously, deciding that this was the best way to thank my grandmother and my parents for all that they had done for me. I made a very tight schedule for myself that began at 6 a.m. with English homework and sports.

The establishment of diplomatic relations with the United States, the growing importance of trade with other countries, and the increasingly frequent visits of expatriate Chinese, had caused everyone to want to learn English. Unfortunately, the rare films in that language that we got to see were poorly subtitled. I liked the "New Wave" films from France. I had heard about the Louvre, but that was all I knew about France.

The courses lasted four hours in the morning and three in the afternoon. In the evening I read or wrote to practice for my thesis. The heroes of my favorite novels – *The Red and the Black, Gone with the Wind,* or anything by Jack London – fascinated me, although they were heavily criticized by Chinese ideologues. I was impressed by their strength of character, which was seen as opportunism by the Chinese. I mourned over *Romeo and Juliet* and shared the despair of the *Lady of the Camellias.* In the evenings we all talked about the books we were reading, so that university life became imbued with romance.

Only the courses on politics and the history of Communism bored me to tears. Since one wasn't allowed to cut them, I took a book to pass the time. However, the number of books that I bought quickly depleted my spending money. My parents sent me thirty yuans each month. Of these, twenty-five had to buy restaurant tickets and the other five were for the books I liked. There was nothing left for day-to-day ordinary expenses, so I had to sneak rides on the bus. I went to see my sister, Mimi, who, overwhelmed with work, took a little time out to slip me five yuans.

Three months after classes had begun, a meeting of professors and students was called, so that everyone could say why they had chosen directing as their future career. Wu Yen, the head of the class, said that he wanted to serve the People, the national culture and the Party and everyone who spoke up after him stupidly echoed him. The professors appeared satisfied with this response. The formal tone of the proceedings made me uncomfortable, even though basically I wasn't opposed to such sentiments. I just felt that something was missing. When my turn came, I sincerely tried to tell how I felt. I explained that I had wanted to choose the most difficult field to prove to my critics that I was a capable person. So I had decided to devote myself to my work above all other things, but I regretted not having any political goal.

The professors looked askance at me, while the class leader's impassive expression told me I had committed a colossal blunder. At the end of the meeting, Kao Lan let me know that I had been stupid to talk like that; I had displeased the professors. Her words were like a cold shower, because her own comments had been rather neutral and, considering her my best friend, I expected her to reject pandering, as I did. She justified herself by saying that the students' fate was in the professors' hands; they were the ones who decided on our job placement. Admittedly she was right, since her parents taught at the university, she knew all the ropes. She predicted that I would be called in by professors because of my comments and indeed the next day I was summoned to the office.

"I've thought a great deal about your comments . . . . I believe that you are here thanks to the Party and thanks to the People who have given you this opportunity. So you must work to thank them. I think that you have too many personal objectives. The cinema must follow the right Party line, don't you agree?"

I explained my feelings: I hadn't had time to think of the People and Party when I passed my exams and I doubted that my fellow students had done so any more than I had. The head professor, a woman, asked me to think about it. These irrelevant suggestions annoyed me so much I pleaded a headache as a pretext for leaving her office.

That evening I preferred not to go to the showing of the

scheduled film. At the dormitory where I was listening to music, I saw Chang Ling come in. She was the one who occupied the bed above mine. I liked her because she was the prettiest and brightest of us all. Nine years older than I, she had all the boys on campus running after her — the very reason why Kao Lan didn't like her. Chang Ling entered the room, her eyes red, and climbed into her bed without a word. When my cassette had finished playing, I could hear stifled sobs. I talked to her, suggesting we take a walk, so that she could tell me what was troubling her.

Since her birth, she had been called a bastard: it was rumored that she was not the daughter of her mother's husband. This gossip was untrue, for her mother, a very beautiful actress, had not deceived her husband. Yet Chang Ling's father had never smiled at his daughter, and his family used her as a housemaid. Her poor mother, who had never been able to disprove the truth of their insults, considered herself lucky that she had not been divorced by her husband. She was unable to protect her daughter, much as she loved her. Finally, Chang Ling could not stand it any longer and enlisted in the Red Guards. One day she led them to her parents' home, which they turned upside down, berating the parents. After that, she moved to the countryside for four years until the Cultural Revolution ended. Knowing that she could never return home after what she had done, she found a menial job sweeping the streets. There she met a crippled shoemaker, fell in love with him and lost her virginity. They lived together as man and wife, lacking only an official marriage certificate, until one day he demanded that they separate. The only reason she could find for this was that he had become tired of her. Since then the luckless Chang Ling had twice tried to commit suicide. But now she was grateful that she had been allowed to get back on her feet and to enroll in the university.

At this point her old lover, jealous of her improved status, sent a letter to the university administration, claiming that her conduct had been immoral and that she had had an abortion. The professors had received this letter a week ago and now they called her in every day to confess. When she refused, they divulged her secret. That evening she had been subjected to Kao Lan's veiled insults and this was the reason for her unhappiness.

I couldn't believe that in the 1980s people would be judged solely on their reputation, in complete disregard of their real worth. Chang Ling had told me the story of her life in confidence, hoping that I would intercede with Kao Lan. I was saddened by the humiliation she had endured and wanted to be closer friends with her. We swore to be like sisters from then on, and strolled for a long time, hand in hand under the trees.

This solemnly sealed friendship fanned Kao Lan's jealousy and resentment toward me. She went so far as to cite a proverb to me, *The wicked stick together like thieves at a fair,* trying to force me to choose between her and Chang Ling. I had no use for a shallow friendship and my choice was easy: I remained Chang Ling's friend.

Gradually, the students broke up into cliques: those from Beijing, others from some particular province, others identifying themselves as "modernists" or "conservatives." As Chang Ling, Hsiao Ch'uan and I were always together, we called ourselves "the odd ones."

As time passed, Hsiao Ch'uan, lively and enthusiastic, funny and generous, made his way into my heart. But I felt guilty because I had sworn not to love anyone after Chou Chiang's death. In order to discipline myself, the more attached I became, the more I avoided seeing him. I succeeded in staying away from him until winter vacation, when Chang Ling, worried at seeing me thin and pale, asked what was bothering me. She made fun of my self-denial, advising me to tell Hsiao Ch'uan about my feelings for him. She had noticed that he had been giving me tender looks.

When my first five months at the university ended, I returned to my parents for the New Year's holidays, feeling that I had learned something about life. My parents had paid for a taxi to pick me up from the station. After a wonderful meal, the whole family, with the exception of Mimi, who had stayed on in Beijing, listened to my adventures. My grandmother was proud of me, declaring that she could now go in peace. Hearing this made me very sad, but it was true that these five months had aged her a great deal. Her bad health cast a shadow on our gaiety that otherwise would have been complete. I begged her to take care of herself. Smiling, she replied that she wouldn't leave before she saw my first film.

Living a sheltered life at the university, I had been isolated from political realities. In the context of "the Struggle against the Pollution of the Mind," an aide of my father's, who also was a friend of mine, was falsely denounced and condemned to seven years in prison, accused of having taken advantage of his position to abuse several young girls. On the other hand, Xu had been freed, thanks to the testimony of his boss. Now he was only waiting for Yen Ying's divorce so he could marry her.

I saw Tien Yeh again; he had made progress in his art, but three years at the university had embittered him. He had just paid a price for showing his canvases on the street: the police had asked him what his motives were. When he told them that he painted when he was feeling happy and when he felt depressed — in short, whatever his mood — these brutes had beaten him with electrified night sticks. They refused to accept the idea that one could be depressed, since the Party claimed to have brought happiness to everyone. So at a time when mankind was sending rockets to the moon, we did not have the right in China to feel sad. According to Tien Yeh, of every hundred Chinese prisoners, sixty were intellectuals, photographers, painters, professors, writers, whose crimes included looking at erotic videos, dancing cheek to cheek, or painting or photographing nudes. Seven years had passed since the Cultural Revolution ended, a period during which the government had never ceased proclaiming how open the country was. But stories like these made a mockery of the official line. The young were frowned upon if they wore jeans or had long hair. Girls were not allowed to wear tight T-shirts and had to tie up their hair. Some older person in the street was always exhorting the crowd to protest young people's subversive hair and clothing. I remember that copies of the Venus de Milo had to be destroyed as indecent, and that Western pop songs were condemned for being too loud and dealing only with love.

The happiest among us was Ta-Chün, who had succeeded in opening his private restaurant. He had even bought himself a motorbike. Nowadays, the police came to see him only to check on his accounts, which were in order. For Tien Yeh, the artist, the pill had been harder to swallow.

This bitter three-week-long plunge into real life made me appreciate even more my return to the bustle of the university. We quickly resumed our impassioned discussions. I was impressed to learn from newspaper articles that in the West young people were freely living together. When they decided to separate, it seemed, they remained good friends, something that was not the case in China. Furthermore, in the West one could have children without being married and without the police intervening — and no one called these children names! Chinese newspapers strongly criticized these attitudes. I found these customs more civilized than ours. According to Chang Ling, many students had secret sexual relationships. A ghost must have eavesdropped on us, for very soon Kao Lan spread the word about my discussions with Chang Ling. It didn't take long for the professors to violently criticize our inclination toward "Western barbarities."

Because of this, I slapped the unbearable Kao Lan twice and, with my best professional technique, won the fight that inevitably ensued. However, no good came of this victory, for I was called to the principal professor's office; it was already decided that I was the guilty one. In fact, I should have known better, since Kao Lan's parents held high positions in the university administration: the decision was bound to go her way.

I was also reproached for making friends with Chang Ling, instead of with the "good elements" in the class. They threatened to notify my parents if I didn't do my public self-criticism the very next day. They had found the chink in my armor — what I feared most was to disappoint my parents.

I remained quiet during the criticism session that followed, where, except for Chang Ling and Hsiao Ch'uan, all my fellow students chimed in with sharp criticism of me, demanding that I correct my behavior. It was a fact that my friend, Chang Ling, didn't have a strong enough voice to be heard over a crowd, while Hsiao Ch'uan claimed a sore throat to get out of the situation, not wanting to anger the professor. The class leader, who got on my nerves, ended the debate with an old proverb: *When you don't know the water's depth, don't step in.*

I told Chang Ling how I felt about Wu Yen, the class leader, but that was a mistake, as she was very taken with him. She insisted that I had misjudged him, that this young man of thirty-two had been a soldier; he was traumatized because he had come within a hairsbreath of death. After eking out a living scavenging in the streets, he had found admission to the university to be like entering paradise. All he wanted was to get along. You could consider him either a go-getter or a manipulator — the choice was yours. Chang Ling and he secretly loved each other, something which bothered me because I didn't think he was good enough for her. Finally, my unquestioning friendship for her led me to try to understand him better.

To punish me for not having spoken up at my self-criticism session, the professors gave me a demerit that was posted on the information bulletin board with my name and my errors in huge black letters, to which the same red seal was affixed that had adorned my letter of admission. Six students shared this dubious honor, due to the Chinese custom of making collective examples. In any case, I was a sort of pioneer: I was the first student of my entering class to receive a public reprimand.

Hsiao Ch'uan treated this whole episode as a big joke. He had a knack for turning my sorrow into joy, my tears into laughter. He was a real charmer. He declared his love for me and to hear him talk, he was born to love me. I was too smitten by his beautiful words to doubt him.

Every weekend we went into the country to have a picnic near a river, under a tree or on a drying haymow. There we grew drunk with dreams, poems and kisses. We gave each other unusual gifts: he offered me books when I gave him flowers; he bought clothes for me when I brought him jam. I learned how to put make-up on and to become a flirt to please him. My skin disorder had healed in the dry climate of Beijing. To my great delight, I had turned white as a lily.

The sixth of May was the dawn of a new year and my eighteenth birthday. Hsiao Ch'uan gave me a stunning gown. For a long time I had avoided this kind of clothing because of the way I felt about my appearance. My parents had sent me twenty yuans: I invited my best friends to a restaurant.

After we had put away seven generous courses and four bottles of liquor, we left, so completely inebriated that we were unable to find our bus stop. When we arrived at a bridge, Hsiao Ch'uan, whose judgement was dulled by alcohol, offered ten yuans to anyone who dared jump into the water. All of us ended up in the canal, including Hsiao Ch'uan himself, who, it turned out, didn't have enough money to honor his bet. Hsiao Ch'uan and I decided to end our evening in a public park. A breeze gently ruffled our hair, while the river murmured and the stars sparkled.

"Niu-Niu, I want you. I've waited a long time."

"Well, here I am. What do you want?"

"But I want to sleep with you!"

I was stunned by his audacity. We weren't married and I didn't see how such a thing could happen. But I remembered my conversation with Chang Ling about the sexual freedom of Westerners. I was tempted. Everything seemed to come together to make this an unforgettable day.

We went to his parents' apartment, and sneaked into his room, not daring to turn on the bedside lamp. Standing on opposite sides of the bed, we took our clothes off before we slid in. We lay there completely paralyzed, each waiting for the other to make the first move. That's how we remained for a few moments, then Hsiao Ch'uan kissed me on the lips, gradually easing himself on me, hesitatingly caressing my body with his hand. Since I didn't know why he was doing this, I thought he didn't know what to do. Our rapid breathing was from fear rather than from sexual excitement. Just as I was thinking that it was all taking an eternity, I felt a violent blow in my whole being, as though my entrails themselves were being torn out. I would have cried out in pain if I had not been terrified of waking his parents. Right after that, he stopped moving and we put our clothes back on.

I was frightened to see that I was bloody. I thought I was going to die. Hsiao Ch'uan was sweating profusely and, just as ignorant as I, was weeping over my impending death. I was equally certain that I didn't have long to live. Hsiao Ch'uan was convinced that I would accuse him of killing me. We decided to write goodbye letters to our parents, saying that we alone were responsible for our act, imploring them not to be sad, as we had died in love with each other. We waited for my last breath and Hsiao Ch'uan's impending execution.

At dawn I was still very much alive and Hsiao Ch'uan, reprieved at the last minute, congratulated himself on his escape. We took the bloody cover with us, so as not to leave any trace, and returned to the university. On the street we were filled with shame, believing that our crime could be read in our faces; we walked with our heads bent, not exchanging a word. I knew that if my grandmother or my parents ever found out, they would die from rage and shame. I had committed a crime against my family — and for nothing pleasurable, to be honest about it. If couples got married just to be allowed to do something so disappointing, the game wasn't worth the candle! Not to mention the fear and the pain . . . .

Two days later, Hsiao Ch'uan, armed with additional information, came to reassure me that I wasn't going to die, something which, in any case, no longer worried me. I had heard that after having sex, some girls became depressed, weeping over it every day. Why such a big thing was made of such an unrewarding activity remained a mystery to me. Nothing had really changed between Hsiao Ch'uan and me, except that we were less at ease with each other. When I told Chang Ling about my experience, she was surprised that I considered the affair of no great interest and that I was not upset.

In fact, my mind was far more preoccupied with the important examination that was going to close the dramatic art course in which each student had to write and perform a brief play. The class was divided into three work groups with a professor for each to direct the rehearsals. Having heard nothing but talk of love affairs lately — Chang Ling's disastrous one, the no less turbulent one of Yen Ying, not to mention my own modest goings-on — I had an idea for a short play on the theme of the persecuted widow. Widows in China have the reputation of having brought bad luck to their husbands. I entitled my project *A Widow Also Has a Right to Live* — an ambitious project that I owed to my romantic temperament.

It was the story of a peasant woman whose husband dies and whose continued bitter existence gravitates between her mother-in-law and her young son. When, however, she falls in love with another peasant, something unacceptable at that time, the entire village, including the mother-in-law, rises up against her. Her lover is beaten to death, she is shunned as a whore. Finally, when she finds her baby dead from hunger and illness, she sets fire to the village before committing suicide. Professor Wang liked my story, and devoted great care to its production.

When the curtain fell, the student audience applauded warmly, but when, a week later, the principal professor announced the grades, mine was the lowest. Indignantly, I demanded an explanation for my low grade, only to be reproached for having written a pessimistic protest play. Its main flaw, I was given to understand, was that it was original.

Professor Wang himself was criticized for permitting me to carry out such a project. He told me that since he was the youngest professor, he was always the first to be blamed. He had tried in vain to get me a better grade. What's more, all the other students in his group had been awarded low grades. Apparently there were as many conflicts among the teachers as among the students, and more was at stake for them. His older colleagues could not allow a younger person to get ahead of them. They would have lost face! Professor Wang explained to me that the same thing was true of salary increases and the allocation of apartments according to seniority. I felt nauseated. Always, educational quality and creativity were being sacrificed.

To console me for my disappointing grade, Professor Wang invited me to an evening at his apartment together with Hsiao Ch'uan, Chang Ling, Ouiyang and others. In the course of the conversation, one of the guests jolted all of us by saying that he believed the Cultural Revolution had had positive effects on the arts and especially on the cinema and theater of the period. Professor Wang pointed out that at least it had wiped out superstitions and ridiculous old customs. I very much appreciated the frank discussions that had enlivened this evening and respectfully thanked Professor Wang for having given me the chance to meet such well-meaning and forthright people.

My only regret at this time was Hsiao Ch'uan's fierce jealousy. He reproached me for being too familiar with the other boys, confessing that his classmates spoke badly of him and had even insulted him for dating a "garbage can." His bluntness made me despondent and for two weeks we did not speak one word to each other. Then, finally, disregarding the custom that demanded the boy take the initiative, I came to him, softening him up with a bit of flattery.

Summer vacation was approaching and each student was supposed to put it to good use by making a documentary. With two cameramen in tow, I planned to follow the course of the Yellow River. My parents, pleased with the project, sent me additional pocket money to add to the budget which the university granted, so that we could live in some comfort.

Southerner that I was, the magnificent countryside of the North enchanted me. I found the cave-dwelling inhabitants especially fascinating. We had envisioned sharing their life, their homes, their strange foods. After three days' walk, we were really in a forsaken hole, where the people stared at us as if we were extraterrestrials. They touched our clothes and our skin, wanting to know what kind of demon our camera was. One of them asked if we had any news of the emperor, coming as we did from the nation's capital. When we told them what was going on nowadays, they refused to believe us and the whole village burst out laughing. I found their poverty and isolation distressing, but their naturalness and simplicity inspired me to do the only thing I could — that is, to produce a good film which, upon my return, I would show them to try and help widen their horizons. When we departed with the material for an original documentary packed away, we left them some money and clothes. This trip enhanced my love for my country, its land and its people. I resolved to work hard to become a good student as my own way of thanking these peasants whose labor provided us with our food and clothing.

Chapter 23
DESPAIR

Back at the university, two other students and I finished editing and mixing our little documentary before handing it in to the professors. As was to be expected, we were given low grades. They considered the background narration inaccurate, the countryside too poverty-stricken and the portraits of the peasants completely unappealing aesthetically. Obviously these idiots thought that we had strayed too far from the Party line. I realized now that any work signed with my name — whether it be a play, a film or a dissertation — would automatically be blacklisted.

After a year of studies, all the students in class knew one another, but paradoxically, each story, each anecdote, each problem was blown out of proportion by our communal intimacy. Tattling was rampant; so was stealing — it was common in the dormitory to hear students screaming that a thief had stolen something from them. Quarreling and swearing were commonplace. Spiteful gossip and meanspirited taunts had taken the place of stirring discussions on subjects close to our hearts.

One day I didn't attend class in the morning because of a splitting headache. I had drawn the little curtains around my bed, when two girls came into the room. They were chattering away about trivia: who was the handsomest boy and so on. Presumably, they had not noticed my presence, so I listened in spite of myself.

The first one said, "I heard that Ping is trying to find a guy."

"Yes, I know and her ex doesn't want her any more because she's let herself go. I have the impression she's slept with Professor Wang, too."

"Ah, good! But which one started it?"

"Maybe it was Ping. Professor Wang is young and very attractive, besides which he has family abroad. Ping comes from the provinces and she really wants to stay in Beijing. It doesn't surprise me that she seduced him. I heard that over the summer she didn't make her documentary and she didn't go back to her family. It seems she went to Shanghai. A professor happened to be there at the same time; he came back yesterday and I hear he said that she behaved badly. The university is going to give her another reprimand."

"I'm all for the reprimand. It's like Niu-Niu carrying on with Hsiao-Ch'uan. What's more, they say that this summer on her trip, she slept with one of the young men. Kao Lan told me that she had told her everything. And Kao Lan has passed it on to the professors — they already have an inquiry under way."

My headache had reached the point where I suddenly had the feeling that I was going to faint. Opening the curtain and getting up, I cried out, "What lies you tell! What are you good for besides attacking people?" My hand brushed against a book and in my anger I threw it at their faces. If I had fallen from the sky, they could not have been more astonished to see me. Shouting threats at them, I pulled my clothes on, intending to go look for Kao Lan.

One of the shrews tried to justify herself. I was disappointed in her, because I had always been friendly to her. Her family was very poor, and she received only fifteen yuans a month, so I had shared clothes, books and food with her. I even lent her money, which she never repaid and which I had not asked for. How could she be so meanspirited? Her behavior made me want to cry. I told her that I knew now how to behave towards her. As is the custom after fights, I demanded that she pay me back what she owed me within three days or I'd throw all her belongings out of the window. Then I stalked out to find her friend and the odious Kao Lan who had lied about me. I wanted a public apology.

The young man whom they had inflated into my lover happened to bump into me just then. "Niu-Niu, we traveled together for a month and a half, so you must have some trust in me. I don't know anything about this story! Why would I tell lies like this? Only girls go in for that kind of gossip."

I soon came upon Kao Lan and in front of everyone I shouted, "Bitch! You can be proud of yourself!" And I slapped her twice. This would have started another fight if Ouiyang, the class chairman, hadn't stopped me.

"Why are you fighting again?"

"Hypocrite! You're the one who's supposed to be the leader of the class and you don't even try to stop all this backstabbing. What's more, you keep your ears open yourself for the latest trashy gossip. Get away from me! Go tell your master that I've had another fight. It'll give you another chance to suck up to him!"

He fled, completely shamed.

The following day I wrote this whole story down to the smallest detail on big sheets of paper that I marked with a red star, mimicking the solemn reprimand of the professors. I tacked one of these to the entrance of the classroom building, another one to the restaurant door, and a third to the official bulletin board. Lots of students stopped to read them, but my pseudo-reprimands didn't last very long. Within two hours one of the professors tore them down and I was immediately summoned to the office.

"You've been fighting again. What was the reason this time?"

"But I said it all in my poster!"

"Why did you make these posters? We have rules here! You've started something again."

"What are you trying to say? Do you really want to know the truth about this situation or do you have to suck up to Kao Lan's mother?"

"Calm down! We're only here to talk. In my position, what else can I do? Anyway, I've already lectured Kao Lan; she admitted that it was her fault and she's going to apologize. Now, let's talk about your problem . . . . I've heard that you are flirting with Hsiao Ch'uan?"

I could see where she was going and I was also sure that she had never lectured Kao Lan. This kind of woman just looks for any opportunity to climb up the ladder. She would never have had the guts to take on Kao Lan's all-powerful mother.

"Madame Professor, what exactly do you want to know? Do you honestly believe that there's a connection between this fight and my relationship with Hsiao Ch'uan?"

"So it's true that you are together. Tell me, what have you done?"

"And you, when you want a young man, what do *you* do with him?"

She threw me a murderous look. Her position as a professor precluded her from blowing up at me. "Now Niu-Niu, I'm trying to have a serious discussion with you. How can you be so crude? This doesn't do you any good. Since you came, I've really had to come to some conclusions about you."

"I have the impression that you've made up your mind

about everyone."

"Be quiet!" She could no longer restrain herself. She was trembling with anger and I was delighted to have upset her.

"Students don't have the right to talk to their professors that way. You fight all the time and your school work shows only bad thoughts. During Saturday class you will do your self-criticism and provide me with two pages of confessions."

"And if I refuse . . . ?"

"Well, you'll get a reprimand."

It was my turn to lose control. "What is this university anyway, these puppets that parade as professors? You blithely twist the truth and make nonsense of freedom." I forgot all that I was risking and leaned toward her. "You're nothing but an idiot, stupid as a headless pig! What can you do besides posting reprimands? Look at your heart and blood! They are black and moldy. How low did you stoop to get your job? If you dare give me another reprimand, I'll really make you sorry!"

In front of her was a cup of tea. I threw its contents into her face. As I left the office, I bumped into Hsiao Ch'uan who had been listening at the door. He was green with fear, begging me to apologize right away. I was beside myself with rage.

"Stay out of this, Milktoast! If you talk to me like that, the only thing you'll get from me is a punch in the nose."

"Niu-Niu, it's for your own good. I'm worried about you. Don't act like a child. Go and apologize to the professor." I was just raising my hand toward him, when the professor came out of her office.

"Hsiao Ch'uan, come see me for a moment."

I glared at Hsiao Ch'uan, trying to stop him from going in; he hesitated, caught between two fires. I grabbed his hand to lead him away from this awful place, but the professor issued a last warning that convinced him. He withdrew his hand, kissed me lightly on the forehead and shamefacedly followed the woman into her office.

I felt disgusted. Hsiao Ch'uan's choice had made me feel worse than if a thousand torturers had beaten me with sticks. Without knowing how I got there, I found myself back in the dormitory. I made a vow never to speak to Hsiao Ch'uan again, the coward! Still, I did love him.

It went without saying that my foolhardiness deserved a rebuke. The authorities brought my mother to Beijing to reprimand me. The poor woman was very depressed. She reproached me, weeping all the while. To her, I had not matured nor made any progress. I tried to justify myself, but it was useless. In order to staunch her tears, I resigned myself to do my self-criticism at the impending general meeting. This brought back old memories of when I was little and had to confess in front of all the schoolchildren. Except for the fact that the Cultural Revolution was supposed to be over, the situation was identical.

One week later my reprimand was in its usual place on the bulletin board when I accompanied my mother to the railroad station, promising her to be good and study hard.

When I came into the dormitory, the girls abruptly stopped talking. I found a pile of anonymous letters on my bed, full of insults: "whore! . . . thief! . . . what do you charge by the night? . . . .this evening the boys' dormitory offers you, tip included . . . ." I forced myself to read the letters aloud in front of the other girls. Hatred and humiliation brought tears to my eyes. I took a cigarette and went to bed, trying to understand why all of them were against me. What had I done to them? Was I really despicable? I took up very little space in this immense country, yet I had the impression that it was still too much.

While these dark thoughts were whirling through my head, I stared at the red tip of my cigarette, so hot, so bright I wanted to press it against me. With masochistic pleasure, I put out the cigarette on my hand. The burning pain made me forget my melancholy as I shrieked in pure satisfaction. The girls ran to me. "Niu-Niu, what are you doing? If you've done wrong, you can improve yourself. We still believe in you! Don't torture yourself like this."

Repelled by their lies, I waved them away. I swallowed my tears, swearing to be strong and brave. When I calmed down, I took my cassette player and some glue and decorated my dormitory door with the insulting letters. "That's better, isn't it? The whole world can profit from these beautiful phrases, just the lovely words a girl likes to hear!"

Two weeks later Hsiao Ch'uan suggested a walk under the trees. "I must speak to you frankly. We have to separate."

I couldn't believe him, searching his face.

"I don't love you any more, Niu-Niu. I can't put up with your nasty temper, and I don't want the professors to be mad at me. You take too many chances and you like to show off."

"Don't say this to me, Hsiao Ch'uan. I know that you love me. I know that in your heart of hearts, you don't want us to separate. Why are you abandoning me when I need you the most?"

"That's the way it has to be. I heard that you received letters, so you know very well what the others think of you. Ever since we've known each other, I have given you all my affection and attention. I've constantly warned you . . . ."

He seemed more unhappy even than I was and couldn't go on. I threw myself into his arms, imploring him not to leave me. He held me very tightly and said in a trembling voice. "Forgive me, Niu-Niu, I know I'm making you suffer, but I feel terrible too — as though someone had stabbed me in my belly. I want to finish my studies in peace and if you love me, you'll help me finish. Say goodbye with a smile . . . . I love you, Niu-Niu."

Swallowing my sobs, I said, "Before you leave, I have one thing to tell you, Hsiao Ch'uan. I love you and before you, no one had touched me . . . . So much the worse for me. So long, Hsiao Ch'uan, goodbye, my love."

It was over. He had gone, I was alone. I walked faster and faster on the playing field until I found myself running . . . . I collapsed on the ground, facing the sky. Why had this happened? I didn't know how I could live and what meaning to give to the word "truth."

The next day in class, Hsiao Ch'uan's eyes were red and swollen. He had wept the whole night. I told Chang Ling about it, but she had already guessed what had happened. From then on, Hsiao Ch'uan and I no longer sat next to each other, and we did not eat at the same table. If our paths crossed, we looked down, pretending that we did not see each other or else we greeted each other with embarrassment. To wipe him out of my memory, I put away anything that could evoke our relationship — books, photos, dresses and gifts that he had given me. I locked them all in my suitcase under the bed.

Nothing was worth so much trouble. I was stupid to be sincere and to take offence at everything that was dishonest. Life was easier for those who did what they were told and I decided to make an effort in that direction. I resolved to become something of a hypocrite, someone who did not say what she thought and would lie whenever it was expedient. When they ganged up on some scapegoat, I would go along. If they stole ten yuans from me, I would steal twice as much from them . . .

My new philosophy bore fruit very quickly. The students came to accept me again. Even the chief professor called me into her office to tell me, "Niu-Niu, you have made progress. You can see that everyone is pleased with you. We believe that you will mend your ways very quickly. As a reward for your progress and upon the recommendation of Professor Wang, we have decided to give you the role of Ophelia alternating with Kao Lan. I think this is a good chance for you to make friends again. I hope you'll appreciate what we're offering you . . . . Oh yes, and another thing. I think it would be a good idea for you to stay away from Chang Ling."

Once again I claimed a headache in order to escape an unpleasant conversation. Still, she was acting very friendly, counseling me to take care of my health in order to study that much harder for the Party and my country.

Rather surprisingly, the promises of the head professor had been the truth, so I began rehearsals for *Hamlet*. Kao Lan tried to resume our friendship, but it was out of the question for me to forgive her and I remained cool. There's a Chinese proverb that's the equivalent of *Once bitten, twice shy!*

Life always keeps some bad jokes in reserve. As though deliberately, Hsiao Ch'uan was assigned to the same work unit as I was. Still feeling unhappy, I took advantage of my role to give my all in tearful scenes. I also intended to prove to the others that, in spite of personal problems, I was above all a real professional. In short, strenuous work seemed the ideal escape for me.

The opening day arrived. Thanks to my efforts and to my breaking up with Hsiao Ch'uan, our group's performance was superior to Kao Lan's, which originally had been scheduled for the majority of performances. The enthusiasm of the student spectators and the support of Professor Wang were enough to favor our troupe, which henceforth performed as often as the other. Every evening the applause made me forget my pain.

After two weeks of performances within the university, the art students gave a large cast party. I saw then that Hsiao Ch'uan had become infatuated with a pretty dramatic art student. To see the two of them smiling and dancing affectionately depressed me and I left the hall at once. As usual, I went out to the playing field to be alone — the very spot where we had separated. It was pretty masochistic, but also a way of writing *The End* to this sad episode.

A shadow came towards me out of the darkness. It was Professor Wang, but what was he doing here? Calmly, he sat down next to me, and asked me what I was thinking about. "I know you've been crying, Niu-Niu. It's because of Hsiao Ch'uan, isn't it?"

"No, it's because of me. I'm sick. I have a headache and a heartache both."

"I can see that. You've changed a great deal these last two months. You've become calmer, you smile less and you go along with the crowd."

"You seem to know everything." I was happy that he was staying to talk to me.

"It's only because I am interested in you. I'm aware of your smiles, your tears, your words, your silence."

His thoughtfulness made me blush, enveloping me with a sense of well-being. Evidently he paid more attention to me than to the other students in his courses. The play would never have been as successful as it was if it had not been for Professor Wang. He had carefully explained the role to me and had me rehearse more often than Kao Lan. And he continually offered me goodies. Flattered, I leaned my head on his shoulder affectionately, as though he were a father or a big brother.

"You know, Professor Wang, I'm bored to death. I'm someone who likes to do things, I crave danger and adventure. These last two months I've tried to conform, but today I feel I can't do it any more."

"But why do you force yourself this way, Niu-Niu? I'm worried about you. I'm afraid that little by little you are consuming yourself. I'm afraid you'll lose your strength of character. You may not know it, but that's what makes you charming. And I really believe that you do your best when you're all stirred up."

I was delighted to hear this and I played along with him by declaiming at the empty stadium, "It is true, Niu-Niu has her emotional moments!"

He looked serious and stroked my face. Then he kissed me on the forehead. That frightened me. When he tried to look into my eyes, I turned my face away. "Niu-Niu, in a short while I'll be leaving to go far away."

The news increased my uneasiness.

"If you're going to paradise, hurry! If it's to hell, save me a place!" He didn't appreciate my banter, and was silent for a while. Finally he announced that he was going to the United States where his grandmother lived. He was only waiting for a visa.

"To the United States! You must be happy!"

"Yes, but I'm concerned about someone who lives in my heart and who keeps me from sleeping. I'm worried about her future . . ."

I thought he was speaking about Ping, who the two gossips in the dormitory said had been involved with him. I was disappointed that he was worried about such an uninteresting girl.

Surely Professor Wang, so brilliant and fine, could have chosen someone more worthwhile. Curiosity made me ask who this person was who was tormenting him night and day. He suddenly seemed hesitant. As I insisted, he suggested I guess.

"It's Ping! I've known this a long time."

"You know nothing at all and you're being idiotic. It's you!"

I fell backwards and almost fainted. "Don't joke about things like this or lightning will strike you."

"I have to ask why the one I love doesn't love me."

"But that's impossible, Professor Wang. I'm your student. And besides, I have this very bad reputation."

"There's never been a law that says a student and a professor can't fall in love. If you don't want to leave for the United States, I'll stay here with you."

This conversation seemed unreal. Professor Wang, whom I respected and looked upon as a father, was declaring his love. I was touched, but I couldn't return it.

"Since your first play, I've thought a great deal about you. I fell madly in love with you, although I knew you were very young and that you were in love with Hsiao Ch'uan. So I watched you and tried to imagine what you were thinking. The night you said goodbye to Hsiao Ch'uan, I was behind this wall. I watched you and I wanted to comfort you. When I learned about the insulting letters, I gave the worst grades to your enemies . . ."

"Why do you love me, Professor Wang, when you know I attract trouble?"

He replied that it wasn't my fault. The society had to change; no one was free at the university. "Niu-Niu, why don't you come to the United States with me? It's a free country where one can do or say as one pleases. Artists aren't chained there . . ."

"I'd love to go, but it's not my country. I don't have friends or family there. I love the Chinese people, I love China, I love my family."

"Your idealism will bring you nothing but disappointment. You'll run into a blank wall."

He was right, all I had to do was look around me, but I preferred to wear blinders. I had never considered giving my efforts and my youth to an unknown country and its people. Like my whole generation, I felt I had to dedicate myself entirely to China.

Professor Wang sensed how I felt and was silent for a moment. At last he asked me how much time I needed to learn to love him. He would be willing to wait, but I wasn't going to lie to him. His gentle fatherly face was not a lover's. At the same time I didn't want to hurt him so I told him that he was a terrific person, and threw myself into his arms to receive his caresses—caresses sweet as spring rain. I was a bit ashamed, but it was so pleasant.

After that night, Professor Wang's eyes never left me in class. At the restaurant, he watched me while I ate. In the evening, he hung around the library where I was studying. I took him aside. "Professor Wang, please stop. You're on the way to ruining your life."

"On the contrary, I enjoy looking at you."

I stammered, "If you wish, we could . . ."

But that was a mistake. He refused, very shocked at my proposition. I wrote him a long letter, asking him to consider me his little sister. I advised him to leave for the United States, where he would discover love and where, some day, I might perhaps meet him to show him the films that I had made . . . . I prepared to mail my letter the night before leaving for vacation. It weighed heavily in my hand, for I assumed that by the time classes resumed, he would have left China. I felt as if I were losing a member of my family.

Chapter 24
THE STUDENTS' REBELLION

We all — Chang Ling, Wu Yen, Kuo Kuo, the student camera-man who had been part of my former crew and I — decided to go to Tibet. One month's vacation and another month to do an off-campus project allowed us the time to make the trip by truck. With my parents' help, we found a transport con-voy, carrying logs, that was taking the same route as ours. We traveled at our own pace, stopping off at charming villages, knowing that, sooner or later, another convoy of trucks would come by.

In one village an old peasant suggested that we might like to take a two days' detour by cart to visit a place still unknown to city people. Even though we were very tired, we couldn't pass up such an opportunity. We went bumping along in a rustic cart over the stony road. Despite our discomfort, we did not regret our journey into this fairy-tale country: an azure-blue lake in the midst of mountains, where two hundred vil-lagers lived in houses set on pilings. There was only one store, which sold salt, matches, candles, yarn and other essentials.

People there worked the fields with buffalo and lived by candlelight in the evenings. They welcomed us with warmth and enthusiasm into their thatched cottages, addressing us respectfully as "city dwellers" or "students." They would gladly have exchanged one of their buffalo for our flashlights and pens. The little mirrors that Chang Ling and I gave the young girls were received as though they were precious treasures. Everyday life there delighted and surprised us.

Chang Ling and I stayed with a family that had seven children three to fourteen years old. With them as guides, we hunted wild fowl and fished from the shore of the lake. We had planned to remain only two or three days, but the place was so enchanting that we spent a whole week there.

One evening, as Chang Ling and I were eating some candy, the seven children were watching us in astonishment. They had rarely tasted sweets, so we gave them each two pieces. The mother collected them all, distributing one piece to each child; the seventh child had to share his with his father. She took none for herself and put the remainder in a locked box. I was deeply moved; it reminded me of my own childhood. We gave them the whole package, placing it in the center of the table. The children sat quietly without touching it, while the delighted mother couldn't stop thanking us.

One morning while we were walking along the fields where peasants were working, we suddenly heard four or five men shouting for joy, waving their arms. Quickly we saw why. In a few minutes their wives came to the field, each one joining her husband. Without wasting any time, the men dropped their pants. The women squealing with excitement while making a show of resistance, very quickly took off their own clothes. There before us, in plain daylight in the middle of the fields, all the couples began to make love. Far from being bothered by the lack of privacy, they turned the whole thing into a contest to see which of the men could last the longest and which of the women could shriek the loudest. The unmarried peasants abandoned their work and became spectators, cheerfully commenting on the amusing activities.

We blushed with confusion, wondering whether or not we should look. Finally we stood there, frozen to the spot. An old woman approached us, smiling. "Well, students, you're blushing?" We were so embarrassed that we took to our heels and ran wildly toward the hills. After a while we stopped, looked at each other and burst out laughing. Quiyang, who was the most worldly-wise among us, explained that in an area as remote as this, making love was the only entertainment, the only pleasure in an austere life; in brief, the oldest and most natural form of amusement. Chang Ling wondered if we should talk about it at the university, but Ouiyang pointed out that people in Beijing would be horrified.

We were surprised to find out that the storekeeper was Chinese. He was forty-five years old and spoke a halting Mandarin. He invited us to visit his home. His wife was Tibetan and they had two children. At his house, the only furniture was a large bed, a stove, a table and a shelf. Quiyang was shocked to see that the works of Mao, Lenin, Stalin and Marx, as well as some well-known novels, served as props for the shelf. Our host explained that the books belonged to him and he told us his story.

He was originally from Beijing. When he was thirteen, his parents, who had been workers, were killed in a traffic accident. An only child, he went to live with his grandmother. When he was twenty-five, a year before the Cultural Revolution, he had been admitted to the philosophy department of the university, where he became the top student. But three years later, because of a dissertation that he had written on the future of Communism, he was declared to be a counter-revolutionary. The university ordered him into exile to a town not far from where we were now, to be reeducated. His grandmother had died in his arms, mad with grief and sorrow. He took everything that he owned to his place of exile. Unfortunately, a year later he protested against an injustice and was labeled politically dangerous. As a result he was banished to this little lost village where he could not speak the language. He fell into a deep depression and then his life changed. When the local storekeeper died, our man, because he could read and count, became the new shopkeeper. "I was lucky," he told us, "because people here did not consider me a dangerous counterrevolutionary. On the contrary, they were very welcoming."

He went on to tell us how one day, when he was struck on the head by a tree he was felling, the village people had improvised a stretcher with branches and straw and they took turns carrying him to a hospital in the nearest town. The village chief's daughter, who had since become his wife, had carried the torch to light the whole long way. Following this accident — which had affected his speech — he had decided to end his days in this village.

"So you've lived here for fifteen years!" exclaimed Chang Ling.

His story touched us deeply. We told him that the Cultural Revolution was over, and many intellectuals were being rehabilitated. We assured him that the Party itself recognized that these ten years had been a serious mistake, that now once again young people had the possibility of going to the university and of studying abroad, that rock and roll and disco were all the rage . . . . He listened, stupefied and his weathered face seemed suddenly to age under the stress that we were causing. When he understood that we were film students, he literally burst into tears.

"You must go see the village mayor and tell him that you are the victim of an injustice and you deserve to be rehabilitated. You must return to Beijing."

But he persisted in believing that he was nothing more than a criminal. Wu Yen got quite irritated explaining that all this was ancient history. Before we left, the shopkeeper came several times to ask us if what we had told him was true. We left him our address so he could come and visit us in the capital. At that, for the first time, we saw him break into a smile as he thanked us profusely. The villagers were very kind, accompanying us part of the way. They had provided us with food for the road and we had left them some clothes, pens, cigarette lighters and flashlights.

We stayed only two days in Lhassa, the capital of Tibet, in order to continue our tour of the interior where other curiosities, like local marriage and funeral rites, awaited us. In one of the villages, Chang Ling had literally bewitched a Tibetan. The poor girl was obliged every morning to swallow mare's milk which the suitor by tradition left outside her tent. If the chosen one refused to drink this curious mixture, the suitor would have to leave the village. His mother had begged Chang Ling to drink it so that she would not lose her son. Besides, it didn't mean that Chang Ling would have to marry him. After a week of this torture, she became ill and we decided to leave. When that day came, the young man followed us on horseback all morning. When we stopped to make our farewells, he remained a few hundred feet behind. This game went on until the driver informed us that if the rider came up to her, Chang Ling would have to decide whether to marry him or not, and if she refused, he would be exiled from the village. The poor young man was therefore paralyzed by the importance of his decision. Chang Ling and I were very touched by this romantic situation; it brought tears to our eyes. Ouiyang, on the other hand, felt left out and jealous; he sulked for two days.

On our way back a month and a half later, we passed through our first magical village again, but the ambience had altered. The peasants closed their doors to us as though we were demons. We wanted to ask the man from Beijing who ran the store the reason for this change of attitude, but his wife insulted us. It seems that two weeks after we had left, her husband had taken his things and all the money in the house to disappear without saying a word. Just as mysteriously, he returned a fortnight later, his clothes in tatters, a blank stare on his face. He later attempted to commit suicide with a kitchen knife; fortunately he was caught in time. Ever since, he refused to work. He burnt his books and spent his days drinking. We would have liked to talk to him, but his wife absolutely forbade us. The village chief advised us to leave as soon as possible and once in the cart, we could see the poor madman watching us from the top of a hillock. It seemed obvious that we had really destroyed him. But what could have happened?

My friends went back to Beijing, while I went to see my parents. Then I took the train back to the capital, where classes were about to begin. Chang Ling met me when I arrived at the station; I was surprised to see Professor Wang with her. I couldn't believe my eyes! He should have been in the United States. I dropped my suitcases and threw myself into his arms. I had never stopped thinking of him during these two months of vacation. I was so happy that he had not left after all. Because his visa was good for three months, he had stayed to say goodbye to me. Impulsively, I said, "I really love you, Professor Wang!" and he, without worrying about the time and place, kissed me on the cheek. He had waited such a long time for these words! That same evening he made dinner for me and, since it was very late, I stayed at his place for an unforgettable night.

He seemed to have grown younger and he always seemed to have a smile on his face. In order to see me more often, he took up teaching again. Our romance became known to everyone and nasty rumors targeted me as someone who had her claws out for Professor Wang just to get to the United States. Actually, I had never really gotten over Hsiao Ch'uan and, in any event, I wasn't sure I loved my professor enough to follow him so far.

At last it was time for Professor Wang to leave. The night before, he invited me to dinner in a hotel for foreigners and at the table asked me if I really loved him. "So, Niu-Niu, why don't we marry?"

To be honest, I had no desire to marry, nor did I want to leave China. I couldn't see myself having children and doing housework. The dinner was rather gloomy: we both were aware that it was the last one that we would have together.

The next day I skipped classes to go with him to the airport. Professor Wang looked downcast. "Write to me, Niu-Niu. You know I'll always be there for you. One word and I'll come back."

"Thank you. But pray to God that doesn't happen."

"You know, Niu-Niu, I'm thirty-five years old, fifteen years older than you. I have the sense of having found the one I love. From the bottom of my heart, I wish for your happiness."

He was weeping as we separated forever. Once more I was losing someone dear, but this time the situation was of my own making. And why, I asked myself, why should someone so brilliant prefer an insecure liberty to life in his own country?

These reflections led me to think that these months of repression were over. I could no longer play a false role. The feisty Niu-Niu had to reappear, even if it killed her. That reappearance occured during an oratorical contest organized by the acting department. Everyone was free to choose his or her own topic. I wanted to express what was in my heart — it took me a month to prepare my speech. I called it "Untitled." Ouiyang, the class chairman, introduced me and I stepped up to the platform. Nervous and emotional, I tried to hide my agitation by taking a good minute to arrange my notes.

Finally I began. "I'm very happy that the professors organized this competition and that they authorized us to choose our own subjects. I'm taking advantage of this opportunity to talk about something that's been close to my heart for a long time.

"My friends and my parents have instilled in me certain principles of tolerance and responsibility. I'm sorry to say that life at this university has failed to live up to these principles. What I want to ask you today is why, since everyone's aim is happiness, we should treat each other so cruelly and spitefully. I have thought that if God exists, it is unkind of Him to force us to submit to the same bitter experience of searching for the answer to this question generation after generation. I do not understand why the old who are approaching death try to tyrannize and bully the young with their old ideas and old customs, why they prevent us from living our lives in our own way . . ."

The students were becoming excited, while the professors were looking cross, but neither group intimidated me. I continued to speak. "Love is the most precious thing. I have been hated, but despite that I have discovered the pleasure of helping someone else attain peace. I hope that we too are going to comfort each other. Think of the old saying, *When one person says something, it is false; when ten people say the same thing, it is possible; when one hundred repeat it, it is true!* That is why we should never speak ill of our fellow creatures, but, on the contrary, combine our efforts to construct a new world."

I had tears in my eyes when I returned to my place. After a few seconds of silence, students began to applaud wildly. One student, who, like me, had received some reprimands, rose to speak. "Niu-Niu is right. We must make a clean sweep of the old values and why not start right now? Let's do it for the sake of everyone's happiness!"

Suddenly some of the students began throwing anything they had at hand into the air — their bowls, their chopsticks, their pens, their books — to show that they were starting this salutary destruction. The professors were waving their arms wildly, yelling, "Calm down, calm down! That's an order!" But no one would listen. I had launched my own student revolt, foreshadowing in its own way the movement of December 1986.

The morning's meeting resulted in classes being called off for the afternoon. In spite of the students' enthusiasm, I was disappointed because they had not understood my message. They had confused material destruction with psychological warfare. At that very moment, Kuo Kuo, the student cameraman, came to sit down next to me. "Niu-Niu, I think that you are going to have some problems."

"Yes, I know."

"Perhaps you should write to your father and ask him to come help you."

The problem was mine, I said, and not my father's.

"You're brave and I honestly hope that nothing will ever dampen your enthusiasm."

"But I'm afraid that is exactly what is going to happen."

Kuo Kuo meant to reassure me, saying that he valued me, gossip notwithstanding, and that he knew others who shared his feeling. Weary and resting my head on his shoulder, I allowed myself to be lulled by his words of comfort. Just then the class informer came in to announce that the director wanted to see me in his office. In the hallway he asked me if I had ever read anyone else's speech. I stopped to look him in the eye, asking him to tell me just exactly what he meant by that.

"I simply wanted to know if you hadn't used this exercise in eloquence to excuse your personal problems. Let me ask you this: how many young men have you slept with?"

"Well, don't forget to list your father and grandfather among them!"

"I'd be surprised if my father would have you."

I had no intention of getting into an argument with this swine. While I tried to calm down, he said maliciously, "At least you won't be defenseless before the director. All you have to do is offer him your services."

That was too much. At the end of my patience, I grabbed him by his shirt to give him the beating he deserved. But it was I who was left on the floor while he stalked off, very proud of himself. I wiped the blood from my mouth and got up like a robot to enter the director's office. He welcomed me in his own way.

"I hear that you have many new ideas and I'd like to know about them, so I can decide if they are worth breaking windows over. You're not saying anything? Good, I gave you your chance; now *I'm* going to do the talking. You've reached the point of no return. You cut classes, you tell others not to join the Party, you criticize the professors. On top of that, you smoke and have a good time. How could anyone possibly say that you deserve to be here? Look what you wrote in your diary: *The university is a desert, a prison, everywhere cold faces and hypocrisy, everything is decadent, nothing is spontaneous . . . ."*

How did he know about my private diary? He told me as if it were a matter of course that a girl from my dormitory had brought it to him. "Your comrades' opinion is your most faithful mirror. That is where you should look at yourself most carefully."

"That is how I have looked at myself a thousand times without finding anything good, anything worthwhile."

"What do you call good? Dancing cheek to cheek, smoking and drinking? Who do you share your secrets with? And by the way, we're looking into your relationship with Professor Wang. You have to give me a detailed report on that relationship."

"Never! You forbid me to love whom I wish and have the gall to read my private diary!"

"Niu-Niu, be reasonable. Your reprimand is already prepared."

"You rotten old egg! You're nothing but a machine to smash the young, a stupid insect. Do you really imagine that I would care about the opinions of the girls who stole my private diary?"

"They brought it in to help you correct your faults."

"You've violated my soul. You'd be better off helping yourself find a mirror that would dare reflect your own dirty, bloated face."

All the professors came running, horrified by my grossness and irreverence: I went on spewing out insults as though I were throwing a pail of piss into their faces. Then, giving the door a kick, I left. The director threatened to have me thrown out the next day. The only reason that didn't happen was because of my father's connections — his going through what was called "the service entrance." He was determined that I should stay at the university.

Two weeks later, my reprimand, as well as that of the boy who had given the signal for the breakage, was displayed on the information bulletin. Next to it were the results of the oratorical contest. Since everyone came to look at these, I had, out of spite, pasted my photo on my reprimand. I stood in front of the bulletin board to offer explanations to the curious. Since I couldn't hope to earn a good reputation, I thought I might as well become notorious.

Hsiao Ch'uan approached me to say he felt bad for me and my parents. "I know that what upsets you most is to hurt your parents. Niu-Niu, I think you deserved to have won the oratorical contest." The director happened to arrive on the scene that moment. Hsiao Ch'uan, like the coward that he was, immediately changed his tone. "Be brave and correct your faults. We have confidence in you and we're willing to help you." The director beckoned, and Hsiao Ch'uan meekly walked away with him. From that moment on, I no longer had even a shadow of feeling for Hsiao Ch'uan.

Kuo Kuo was the one who was most sincere in comforting me. He sounded like Chou Chiang, Yen Ying and Professor Wang — all those who had encouraged and inspired me, but were no longer with me.

Again I was showered with insulting letters, but felt nothing. Once again I stubbed out a cigarette on my hand, but that wasn't painful enough. I decided to go further, ready for anything to escape the hell that was my university life. I took a knife; I was going to cut my wrists. It seemed like my only escape.

Then I changed my mind.

Chapter 25

AN UNWORTHY ROLE

Three reprimands in two years was a record. I had become a character on campus; everyone called me "the bad girl." I only went to class when I felt like it; I didn't bother to prepare and sat there reading a book. The professors had already made up their minds about me — they were satisfied as long as I remained quiet and didn't start any disturbances. I knew that they would not award me a diploma at the end of my studies, not even a letter of recommendation to help me find work.

Aside from Chang Ling and Kuo Kuo, no one came near me. Gradually I began to spend less time on campus, where I was ostracized. Among my new friends were businessmen who opened my eyes to life outside the university. This is how I came to know Ho Wei. His father was a big shot and thanks to his protection, Ho Wei could engage in any sort of illicit trading. He was nice and generous with me, so that I didn't hesitate to give him a phone call whenever I found life at the university more than I could bear.

I also made a new girl friend, a student in film editing who already had two reprimands to her credit, which made her a bad girl like me. We gave each other foreign first names; she became "Nancy." One evening while we were waiting to meet a friend at a hotel, two Chinese men approached us. Since the only Chinese allowed in this type of hotel were businessmen and high government officials, we had no qualms about talking to them. The friend we were waiting for didn't show up, so we accepted their invitation to dinner.

Later, when we went dancing in a disco club, our two escorts, without taking their eyes off Nancy and me, went to talk with two Chinese guys from Hong Kong. When the four of us were getting into the taxi that was to take us back to the campus, the two strangers, looking very cross, began to argue with the men we were with. Once the driver had shut the car doors, one of our companions told him, "You'll get a big tip if you lose the taxi behind us."

What followed was like something out of an action film. Our car took off down the dark and narrow streets of Beijing, while the guys from Hong Kong chased after us. At each red light we came within a hair's breadth of tragedy, until finally we lost the other taxi. I had an inkling of what was going on. Without the slightest embarrassment, our Chinese explained that the two others had paid to spend the night with us.

In spite of her humiliation, Nancy couldn't resist asking how much they had paid. "Two hundred Hong Kong dollars for each of you." I was furious that they had considered us whores. "Don't get so mad. After all, we didn't deliver on it. If we had, would we have gone in this taxi with you? We only meant to teach these Hong Kongese a lesson. These morons think their dirty money can buy anything in China."

I threatened to denounce them to the police, but as they knew everyone there, the situation would only have been turned against me. They didn't even want the money and offered to give it to us.

"Shut up and keep it to buy your mother's coffin!" In my anger I slapped the one seated next to me. He would have retaliated if Nancy had not had the presence of mind to tell him that I was a friend of Ho Wei's. This stopped him immediately.

Early the next morning, I phoned to tell Ho Wei what had happened. A week later, he let me know that I could rest easy: he had ordered his "soldiers" to teach the two creeps a lesson. I was delighted that Ho Wei could protect me, but I was curious to know the nature of his little business. Since the reopening of China to foreign trade, companies of all kinds had proliferated, with the businessmen treating themselves to nice meals and elegant evenings. Some Chinese, like Ho Wei, had become amazingly rich.

He had studied in Switzerland for four years and when he came back he became the director of a state enterprise. He had been content with his salary until he noticed that his boss was carrying on a little enterprise of his own, using the company's facilities. Beginning to catch on, Ho Wei teamed up with sons of other high officials, who were dealing in cars and motorbikes. Didn't Deng Xiaoping, the new Chinese leader, encourage people "to prosper and grow rich"? Ho Wei also made himself useful by expediting authorizations needed by businessmen for importing equipment. His power had increased with his wealth. In Beijing, he had established his own spheres of influence, though these were not easy to maintain. There were daily fights between rival gangs, with no holds barred, to take over successful rackets or at least to mess up a rival's operation.

Ho Wei's brother had disposed of ten Japanese cars that had originally been acquired by an opposing gang. One evening, somewhat drunk, he took a taxi; the driver turned out to be a member of a rival gang he had cheated. The brother was taken hostage and forced to pay ransom; they had held him for four days but they had not mistreated him because he was a gang leader and the underworld observed its own rules. Nevertheless, Ho Wei's brother waited less than a week before he stole several vehicles from his abductors in order to recoup the ransom money. When trafficking in cars became too complicated, Ho Wei decided to trade in antiquities, although that was dangerous too. One antique deal brought in as much as selling ten cars.

Ho Wei looked so upright that I could hardly believe what kind of man he was. He told me that a friend of his, whose father was not as highly placed as his, had been trafficking in gold. When the police investigated him, he was condemned to death as an example. All his money and property were confiscated and his parents made to pay for the bullets used in their son's execution.

I worried about Ho Wei's future, but he had evidently anticipated everything: he had already bought a Japanese passport and had had a bank account in Tokyo for a long time.

The world outside the university amazed me; it seemed to defy all logic. The repulsive way of life that Ho Wei told me about disgusted me to the point that I decided to see less of him. When all was said and done, artists and writers were less perverse. However, my decision was put on hold when Ho Wei redoubled his attentions to me and plied me with gifts. One day he brought me chocolate, the very thing that I hate most in the world, for its taste reminds me of the medicine I had had to take to clear up my skin disease. I distributed it to the girls in the dorm, who decided to be nice to me again. They asked me to treat him well and they seemed happier than I was when he arrived loaded with presents. But he ignored them, finding them vulgar and selfish.

"How could you live here for two whole years with these shrews?" His question, which seemed like a reproach, made me uncomfortable. Not only was it intolerable that this gangster dared criticize my way of living, but even worse than that, he was basically right. He suggested that I take part in some of his business deals to improve my situation, but I made it obvious that I would prefer death to participating in his shady affairs. We became angry with each other. Our discussion ended in a quarrel, which he cut off in his own inimitable way by saying, "You're really adorable, Niu-Niu. Come on, tell me what I can offer you with my dirty money that would please you."

I had to admit he had a great personality, always saving the situation with humor. I promptly replied in the same tone. "There are at least a hundred books that I've been looking to buy for a long time."

The next day I had them. Although the power of his money made me uneasy, I had to recognize that I was also envious of it — an insight that was a blow to my idealism. One day he invited the girls from my dormitory to a restaurant; all of them arrived decked out like starlets, thanks to Ho Wei's generosity. But I could not forget that the source of his money was immoral. "You know, Ho Wei, you lead me to believe that the whole world is corrupt."

"Don't be childish, Niu-Niu, be realistic. Admit that what this university teaches you amounts to a good lesson in what not to do. I love you a lot, Niu-Niu! You remind me of a lotus, a beautiful flower growing in the mud. . . but sometimes I'm amazed at how naive you are."

While we were dancing at the disco with Ho Wei's pals and the girls from the dormitory, I saw some very chic Chinese women who were dancing and seemed to chat naturally, without embarrassment or reserve. I asked Ho Wei if they came from Hong Kong, but he told me that they were prostitutes from Beijing. I was upset that he didn't know the difference between modern young women and prostitutes.

"But I'm telling you, Niu-Niu, they walk the streets. I even know their names. When we opened our borders, these poor girls found out that by sleeping with foreigners they could get paid in foreign currency that bought what the People's money couldn't buy. They can't find other work and if they do, they are paid less than half of what they can earn in one evening. If they are smart enough to convert their currency into Chinese money on the black market, their worries about making ends meet are over."

While I believed that some of them were searching for love or were simply out to have a good time, he saw only the sordid side of things. Ho Wei tended to agree with everything that I said, which made me feel even more uncomfortable, because objectively he knew more about life than I did. I was saddened at the thought that these pretty girls, who whirled around the dance floor like blithe spirits, demeaned themselves for money. It was depressing. Since the Liberation of 1949, prostitution had officially disappeared, but right here, under my stupefied gaze, prostitution was rife in this luxury hotel.

I was confused by the venality of the world outside the university. I had attempted to leave an environment that I thought corrupt and hypocritical, only to lose myself in another one even more disheartening. Did love and friendship no longer exist or did my naiveté blind me to reality? Why, then, had God wanted me to know such wonderful people as Yen Ying, Chang Ling and Professor Wang? Why had He wanted my parents to be artists who had the purest motives in life? Why had He given me a grandmother with a big heart to foster generous principles in me? I was overwhelmed by all this, as diverging roads opened up before me. My childhood dreams were coming apart, one by one.

So I began to change. I changed the way I thought about things; I became bitter and callous in the process. To protect myself from others, I was filled with hate and I didn't trust anyone. I knew what I wanted and if this took money and flattery, so be it. All I had to do was go with the tide: I wasn't going to resist outside pressures any more. I began to smoke and drink too much. I stopped worrying about finding love and slept with Ho Wei, taking the gifts and pocket money that he gave me. I went wild and cheerfully passed gifts out to the girls in the dormitory, which also meant that I could ask them to leave whenever I wanted to be alone. My life was an open book; I no longer had any modesty or shame. Sometimes when I ran out of money, I sold one of Ho Wei's gifts — the watch, the gold ring, the bicycle — to buy myself cigarettes or drink or to go dancing.

He lived in a large apartment, something very rare in Beijing. Since I found it much more comfortable than the dormitory, I spent entire weekends there. Ho Wei would pick me up in his car, and take me back on Monday morning. One day he asked me the fateful question. "Niu-Niu, do you love me?"

"No, not at all!"

"Then why do you sleep with me?"

"Because I want to — and then because you have money. Have you forgotten how you told me that it was the key to everything? So you see that I've adapted."

After a while I began to get tired of this dissolute life, but I had no alternative. One morning when Ho Wei deposited me at the campus entrance, Kuo Kuo was standing there glaring at me. When the car disappeared, he came over, took me by the arm and led me to the playing field, where he began to scold me. He said that I was lost, that I deserved my nick-name of "Bad Girl," that I was rotten to the core, that I had to stop smoking and drinking, that he could no longer stand see-ing me so blasé. "You don't know it, Niu-Niu, but when you drink too much, you get completely obnoxious."

"Get lost! It's my life, it's not your problem. You have no right to insult me."

"I do have a duty. I can't let you go on ruining yourself. I know you don't want to hear this, but I remember, Niu-Niu, how charming and pure you were when you first came here two years ago. You were full of courage and hope! You've thrown all that away. Look at what you've done with your life, you seem completely dead. Reread the plays and sketches that you produce nowadays — they're trash! And the more you sleep with Ho Wei . . ."

"Stop, Kuo Kuo, please! Don't rub it in."

"I can't help it. You don't know how much I love you and want to help you. Don't you have any regret? Have you for-gotten what you said in your speech?"

He had cut me to the quick, his criticism overwhelmed me with shame. He was not mistaken: there wasn't a day that I hadn't wanted to recover my idealism, not a day when I didn't want to go back to being innocent again.

"It's not my fault, Kuo Kuo. You're right, I'm a slut. But I've been badly hurt."

Trembling, I took out a cigarette. Kuo Kuo snatched it out of my mouth, shouting that I must stop smoking. "Your tongue is black with nicotine. Tobacco and liquor don't solve anything. They're not going to make you happy. Niu-Niu, please, get hold of yourself. Fight the professors and try to convert the students. I'll help you. I'll be there with you."

"How can I have confidence in anyone again? So many

promises made and none kept. I feel wretched and alone."
We wept together. Kuo Kuo seemed as much at a loss as I did;
he stroked my hair to soothe me, giving me a bit of the comforting that I so badly needed. He apologized for upsetting
me; he said that he just couldn't bear seeing me like that.

"I don't know that I can change, " I said. "I don't have the
strength. I'm worn out and I feel terrible wherever I am."

"It's a question of will! You're not exhausted, you're lazy
and you're letting yourself go."

"No, everything's finished for me. I really don't want to fight
any more."

He pushed me away, saying furiously, "All right then, bury
yourself in the mud, if that's what you want." He let go of my
hand and ran off as fast as his legs could carry him.

"Come back, Kuo Kuo! If you don't come back by the
count of three, I'll kill you!"

He didn't return. I went back to the dormitory and swallowed enough sleeping pills to end it all. The girls in the dormitory found me in time and my stomach was pumped out at
the university hospital. I convinced my professors not to notify my parents that I had attempted suicide. During my week
of convalescence, Kuo Kuo came to bring me little good things
to eat that he had made on the dormitory hot plate. He asked
me to be his girl, but I refused; I no longer had any interest in
loving anyone.

One more week and we would be on vacation. I had been
so shamed and wounded by Kuo Kuo's words, that for the
last three weeks I had not talked to Ho Wei. He had continued to phone, but with Chang Ling's help, I had succeeded
in avoiding his calls. I told her to tell him that I didn't love
him at all and didn't want to see him any more. She was terse
and convincing where I would have faltered.

One evening I was quietly reading in bed. At eleven o'clock the lights were turned off as they were every night at that time. I heard Ho Wei calling me from beneath my window. He sounded breathless. I knew at once that this was an emergency, so I dressed and ran outside.

His pale face reflected his fear. He asked me to get into his car so that we could park in a secluded place. He was in trouble. Two weeks ago his father had retired and, inevitably, the police had taken advantage of this to look into Ho Wei's affairs. The police knew all about him and already had a warrant made out for his arrest — it only needed their chief's signature.

"But what can I do for you? I have no influence with the powers that be."

"Don't worry, I've planned everything. Tonight I'm going to another city and tomorrow I'll be taking the boat to Japan. I only came to say goodbye."

"But you're completely crazy! It's much too risky!"

"I know that you never loved me, but I really do love you. I've never taken women seriously, but I'm serious about you. Listen to me, Niu-Niu. After I'm gone, you have to be careful. Don't go to the hotels for foreigners too often. They're full of thugs and plainclothes police."

I couldn't have imagined that he would think of me at a time like this. He seemed terror-stricken, he kept nervously looking around to make sure that we were alone. "Now I do have a favor to ask you, since you're the only person that I really trust. Here, take this little suitcase. It's full of dollars and gold. The police will search my apartment and my parents'. Would you mind keeping it for a week? My brother will come and get it."

"But the police may get to me!"

"I swear to you that no one knows where you live, aside

from my brother. I beg you to help me. Look, I'm leaving — there won't be anyone here to take care of you — I'm giving you two thousand yuans."

He was desperate, so I agreed to hide his suitcase. But I wouldn't accept the two thousand yuans. I thought he might need them, but he pushed them into my pocket, drove me back to the university, thanked me and left. In spite of my disappointment in him, I hoped that he would make it to Japan.

I couldn't sleep that night because I was holding the little case in my arms under the covers. I waited until the girls had left to hide it in a large suitcase against the wall. Thereafter I didn't dare leave and was stuck in the dorm while I waited to hear from Ho Wei's brother.

Two days later he arrived without calling first. Ho Wei and I had agreed on a password, so I knew he was the one I was waiting for. I gave him the attaché case plus the two thousand yuans, and told him not to come see me again. Before he left, I asked if Ho Wei had made it. "All's well. In two weeks' time I'll join him!"

Evidently if you had a father in high places, everything was possible. And when the father lost power, money could replace him. Maybe if my father had been rich and influential, my luck would have been better. Well, so much the worse for me! I myself was going to leave in another two days, not to the Land of the Rising Sun, but to visit my parents. Of the four years at the university, half were already behind me.

Chapter 26
THE FOREIGNERS

I stayed only three weeks with my parents, because Kuo Kuo and I were to meet in a city north of Beijing to film a documentary. Unfortunately, stopping in the capital, I learned that Kuo Kuo was ill and that I would be alone until the end of vacation.

I took advantage of being at loose ends to wander about, and that is how I came to make the acquaintance of a number of foreign students and residents. They were likable and polite and with them I didn't encounter the usual insults and pettiness; they seemed to be happy, satisfied people. I did find their taste in clothes a bit jarring. Even older women wore bright colors. They weren't afraid of anything, some even kissing on the mouth in public. And then, I didn't understand why the authorities of their countries allowed them to travel freely all over the world. Weren't they afraid that they would sell secrets to the enemy or run away? They stayed in luxury hotels and moved about only in taxis. Their wealth literally exceeded the comprehension of the average Chinese. I also didn't understand why we didn't have the right to enter into "their" hotels; it was as though things hadn't changed since the 1930s when such places were "forbidden to dogs and Chinamen." Of course, such signs were no longer being posted by foreigners. Today these prohibitions were mandated by the Chinese government itself.

Foreigners were harshly denounced in the local papers as carriers of AIDS, drug addicts, immoral people who misled young Chinese. My friend Nancy, for example, was considered to be a whore just because she was acquainted with some foreigners.

My curiosity grew, so I dressed myself like a girl from Hong Kong in order to enter places reserved for foreigners. In the course of conversations, I learned that Westerners had a good deal of freedom. They seemed to be honest and I wanted to believe their stories. They told me that in their countries no one had the right to stick his nose into other people's business. Even adolescents eighteen years old no longer lived under their parents' authority. In short, I discovered that not all of them were addicts or victims of AIDS. This encouraged me to get to know them better.

I met David, an American with a good sense of humor, who was working for a foreign company. He often invited me to lunch or to take a trip to the outskirts of Beijing on his motorbike. One evening, at the end of a party, I found myself in his room. This was the first time that I had kissed a foreigner, and it seemed bizarre and disagreeable. I couldn't stand his tongue in my mouth; I asked myself why he did that. I stubbornly kept my mouth shut. When we made love, it was like a nightmare. I felt I was being raped.

Somewhat later, I became afraid of being pregnant and, feeling helpless, I telephoned him for advice. He asked me if I was sure that he was the only one who could be responsible. Not only did he humiliate me, but he had the nerve to warn me that marriage was out of the question. It didn't occur to me to blackmail him, but the shame he had caused me prompted me to pay him back.

Thanks to Chang Ling, I was able to find a doctor who told me that I wasn't pregnant. Secure in the good news, I went to find David to make him sweat. "I know a doctor who'll do an abortion for me for two thousand yuans." He turned pale which pleased me. Then I frightened him by telling him that if he did not give me this money, I would denounce him to the police and the authorities would force him to marry me or have him imprisoned to set an example. He gave me the money on the spot. He had it coming, despicable man that he was! Yet my victory was spoiled by the knowledge that he had a very low opinion of Chinese women, so my little trick, of which I was not proud, did nothing to improve his attitude.

One day I was invited to have dinner with a foreign student, a young woman. The hotel doorman stopped me, asking for my name and why I was coming there. "What work unit do you belong to?" I knew that if I answered honestly, he would call my university immediately — which would cause me cata-strophic problems.

"I didn't bring my work certificate with me."

He persisted in barring my entry. When I saw another Chinese girl go in with friends, I demanded to know what the difference was between us.

"She's a Chinese from the West."

"Why do you act this way against your own people? You should be ashamed!"

"I'm not interested in arguing. I'm the one in charge of guarding this door today and you will not enter. And further-more, the more you irritate me, the less chance you'll have of getting in."

Thanks to the energetic intervention of my Western friend, I finally got in, but I felt uncomfortable that it had taken a foreigner to force him to agree. Then I had a brush with the waitress in the restaurant. After I had politely asked her to serve me, considering that my friend's meal had arrived thirty minutes earlier, she squinted contemptuously. "What are you interfering for? You think you can give yourself airs just because you're having dinner with a foreigner?" Fifteen minutes later, she literally threw my plate on the table, while I tried to calm my friend who was ready to call her every name under the sun. That waitress should have been satisfied with her life, since working in a hotel was the dream of all young Chinese.

At the university the students had spread the word that I was seeing some of these foreign devils. I was called into the office. According to the professors, I had a problem because I was trying to be friends with "those people." There were, I was told, plenty of Chinese — you didn't have to look elsewhere.

"What's the matter with foreigners? Aren't we all brothers?"

"We want to warn you, Niu-Niu, you'd better keep your self-respect and not lose your Chinese soul. If they turn out to be dishonest with you, who would you complain to?"

"Why do you imagine that foreigners are so bad and that a Chinese loses face rubbing shoulders with them? It's this way of thinking that shows a lack of self-respect!"

"We don't want to discuss this with you any more. If you're going to be stubborn, the university won't tolerate you within its walls."

Walking toward the dormitory, I ran into Kuo Kuo who told me the girls were saying that I earned money sleeping with foreigners. "Be careful, Niu-Niu. It would be better to put an end to these indiscretions.... You know if you need money,

I can give you some."

He was worried about me, but he was really tactless: I couldn't forgive him for his suspicions. Nevertheless, I found myself in a delicate position. Chang Ling told me that the Chinese had become xenophobic because they had been humiliated over the course of their history. According to her, this old hatred had a tight hold, even if foreigners were allowed to live in our country again now. The Chinese, afraid of losing face, were jealous of the foreigners' luxurious style of living.

I had learned a lesson. I had to be careful. I decided to dress Hong Kong style and speak only English when I went into hotels—to play at being a foreigner in my own country. Then I heard that police had raided the rooms of one large hotel and arrested all the Chinese women they found there. These women were sent to a reeducation camp in Xinjiang; those who were students were expelled from their universities. That cooled me off for several weeks.

It quickly got to the point where I found all this unbearable. No one understood me in this country and it was with great astonishment that I had to admit to myself that the day predicted by Professor Wang had arrived. My youthful dreams and hopes were vanishing in smoke. I had to flee this inhospitable land, leave this sun and air where I had grown up. Tearfully I decided to leave it all.

 Chapter 27

TAKE OUT YOUR HANDKERCHIEFS

A short time after I had decided to leave, I received a long letter from my mother. I needed some comforting; unfortunately, this was not a comforting letter.

> My dear Daughter,
>
> I hope that you're in good health. We miss you a great deal, but we are worried about you. We know what goes on in Beijing. I would have liked to write earlier, but my work prevented me.
>
> Why don't you write to us? Are you having such a good time that you forget your family? We think of you every day. We wear ourselves out, we even neglect our health, to make more money to send to you and your sister. Even when we are dead tired, it is reward enough for us to think that you're doing well in your studies to become a film director.
>
> Nevertheless, I have the impression that my hopes are not materializing, because you're acting like a scatterbrain. I and others here have been told all about your foolish behavior in Beijing. They have finally found a good opportunity to insult your parents, "these two imbeciles who pull strings for their good-for-nothing daughter. . . ."

Niu-Niu, I'm upset with you and your Grandma is just sick about it. Even your little sister doesn't dare to talk about you any more. And your father, who is always ill during the winter, has had to stop filming because he couldn't sleep worrying about you. He urged me to write and tell you not to inflict all this shame on us, not to make us lose face, to beg you to be sensible, not to associate with people from outside the university, to be studious and work hard to the end of the semester. After that, you'll come back home. Making films demands maturity and intelligence, qualities which unfortunately you do not yet possess.

Niu-Niu, your parents love you from the bottom of their hearts, especially your father. Of his three daughters, you are his favorite because he looks upon you as a son; he hopes for great things from you. Not a day goes by that he doesn't speak of you. Since he found you again, he has always kept asking your grandmother to tell him all about your life during those eight long years.

But Niu-Niu, now you are causing him a lot of grief. Your father doesn't like to cry, but he is shedding many tears. Do you know that? You are the one who has caused most of the troubles in our family. Moreover, you don't seem to learn from your mistakes and you don't apologize so that you can be forgiven; little by little everyone is losing patience with you. What good does it do to behave like that? When you were young, your parents could still help you and teach you, but now that you are on your own, you hold your life in your own hands. Why are you constantly working to wreck your future? Why do you always keep putting obstacles in your own path?

You will be twenty years old soon and you won't be able to pass off making an ass of yourself as youthful folly, or ask that bygones be bygones. I had hoped to have highly intelligent daughters, but I can't be proud of you. You requested that nothing about your behavior be reported to your parents, but around here they don't spare us their sarcastic remarks.

Niu-Niu, life is beautiful and interesting. How could you be heartless enough to swallow those pills, to abandon life and leave us? Your parents, in spite of their white hairs and wrinkles, enjoy life more every day, working hard to accomplish interesting things before they disappear from this earth. You, so young, are you already sick of life? Is it true that you are ill and weak and that's why you have sunk so low? How can we help you? Tell us. We would rather die than be kept in ignorance. You probably don't know how much we love you; in spite of everything, you are our daughter. There are children in the world who do not love their parents, but there are no parents who don't love their children.

My daughter, my little Niu-Niu, if you feel any affection for us, if you wish to make us a little bit happy, listen to my advice. Stop these excesses, plunge seriously into your studies, start over again. Don't make your grandmother and your father ill, and above all don't go out any more with men you don't know.

Make the most of your youth and try to accomplish interesting things. I cannot do anything more than pray to God to show you the right direction. I impatiently await your letter.

I love you always.

Mama

P.S. Now that I have reread my letter, I want to tell you to memorize it and then burn it. The most important thing is our security in case someone gets hold of our letters, something which has already happened.

As I was reading my mother's letter, I imagined her weeping as she wrote, by the light of her desk lamp. I saw, too, my grandma's eyes, grey and opaque, reflecting the sadness I had known in my childhood. My father seemed to be whispering, "Are you waiting for me to weep blood for you?"

Tears were running down my cheeks, my heart was beating as if a thousand needles were piercing it and I was shaking as if my body were ready to come apart. I was ashamed and I despised myself bitterly. I had fallen into the worst depravity, but how could I get out of it? Was everything really my fault?

Several days went by without my having the courage to dry my tears or to take up my pen. Only Chang Ling, my sworn sister, knew my state of mind and I let her read the letter in spite of my mother's admonition.

"Niu-Niu, your parents are really good to you. It's the thing that I have missed most in the world. Now you have to answer them. I'm sure they'll understand you. Stop crying; you're the only one who can do something about it."

I established myself in an empty classroom, placed some candles I had just bought before me and got ready for a sleepless night in order to answer my parents.

My dear Parents,

I think about you a great deal. After reading your letter, I wept and cursed myself. I am ashamed and no longer know what to do to deserve your forgiveness. I have been living on my own now for almost three years and I'm standing on my own two feet. During this period I promised myself to study hard, to make good films, so that one day you would be proud of me, so that you would never be upset.

But the university has not let me do this. On the contrary, it has stifled me and overwhelmed me with despair. You should know that the big mistakes which they held against me and for which I earned three reprimands, were being sincere, speaking frankly and helping someone else.

Of course, these are the things that you taught me to do, but unfortunately they are not respected here, my dear parents and grandmother.

The professors don't try to understand the students, and they don't care about their talent. Here everything is gossip and denunciation. A friend of mine asked me the other day, "Where is freedom? Where are the pure of heart? Why does it take so much hypocrisy to succeed? Why is it that those who started out brave have become cowardly? And why do the cowards grovel like cockroaches?"

You see that I'm not the only one who finds things rotten here. I am not trying to excuse myself, but I have to tell you what is upsetting me.

You accuse me of having shut you out of my life, but I never intended to deceive you. I am nearly twenty and I have my own lifestyle now. I only wish that my problems would not fall on your shoulders. That was the only reason I did not want you to know that I had swallowed sleeping pills, or that I had been insulted.

My dear mother, when one is young, one has countless dreams and unlimited courage to do great things. You must know that I have always loved fighting my demons and saying what I pleased — it must be hereditary. This is what has caused me all these difficulties. I'm confused by the troubles I seem to attract. I was following your example in trying to help others, without hypocrisy, while trying at the same time not to make my superiors jealous. As you yourself have done in your life, I tried to make some progress in mine. Yet all my attempts to be kind and to show good will have brought me only abuse and sarcasm.

Suddenly I find myself alone, with no one to understand me, even among people my own age. Hsiao Ch'uan and Chang Ling were the two friends I loved most in the world, but then one left me, while the other has grown silent and fearful.

My dearest parents, you must know that I am not someone who gives up or who hides behind deceit. You're fond of old proverbs, telling me over and over again that the hunter kills the first bird to leave the tree, but I don't care about these old saws, even though I have been winged by the hunter's bullets. I don't like to lose, and I can't bring myself to raise my hands in surrender. You keep accusing me, but what have I done? I don't understand.

Mama, Papa, I know you love me and I love you, but sometimes this strong love frightens and stifles me. I hesitate to act for fear of giving you new reasons to be upset. That is why I made myself write out my self-criticism and read it aloud. You must still remember that. Evidently this was not enough and since then I have changed my life, no longer behaving the way I thought was right. I'm no longer the real Niu-Niu.

I can't do anything more. I'm tired. I've had enough. My soul is bitter. No one hears my cry against injustice. Others have cast shame on me and you your-selves have renounced me. What else could I do but take the pills? It's not that I don't love life, it's that life rejects me.

I remember that every year on my birthday, Grandma took me to the abandoned temple to pray to Buddha to protect you. She would say to me, "Niu-Niu, in all the world, it's your parents who love you the most. You also must love them very much. Don't forget to do all that's possible to make them happy and proud of you." I have always remembered and I always will.

All I ask is that you allow me to take my own path, even at the risk of seeing me stumble.

I love you so much. If one day you were to pass away, only half of Niu-Niu would be left. That's all I have to say. I have told you frankly how I feel. I love you always.

My hand was aching and my eyes were puffy when daylight streamed through the classroom windows. The sunrise soothed me. Having finally opened my heart in the hope that my parents would understand and forgive me, I sent my let-ter by express mail.

For two weeks I went at regular intervals to the caretaker's office. Finally he handed me a letter. I could hardly stand it when I saw that the writing on the envelope was my father's.

My poor Niu-Niu,

My dear daughter, I received your letter and I think that we have not been fair to you. Today I'm asking you to excuse our strong words. In the future, we are going to try harder to understand you. Do the same with us and everything will be all right.

Since we found you and Grandma again, Niu-Niu, I couldn't help but think of you as my favorite daughter. You remind me of myself when I was young, and if I have hurt you, it's because I put a father's highest hopes on your shoulders.

You remember the essay that you wrote in high school when you were fourteen? Its title was, "My Greatest Hopes." In it you said that you wanted to be an eagle with powerful wings and sharp talons. I still keep this locked in my drawer; I often read it when I miss you. It probably influenced the way I raised you. I took you with me when I was filming, and to the showings at my studio. When I was talking about work with my young colleagues, you were there. I was delighted to see you sitting there with us, listening thoughtfully. Your strong personality made me want to help you. Do you remember when I saw your letter of admission from the university, I stood at my studio door, bragging to everybody who went by? I was so proud of you.

You resemble me so much: intelligent, kind, considerate toward others. . . . but you have also inherited my bad traits. You like to have a good time, you are impulsive and unrealistic. When the choice is between your emotions and your reason, your heart takes over. These are good qualities for an artist, but dangerous in everyday life.

Niu-Niu, I know about Chou Chiang and Hsiao Ch'uan. Love brings happiness, but sometimes also despair. I have experienced that. Don't use up your resources. Be strong and take the long view. Don't take the shadow for the substance. Use your older sister as a model; she never lets grief get her down. I myself have never stopped struggling. Shouldn't you then do as much?

For all that, Niu-Niu, don't be afraid of falling in love, for one day you'll find your soulmate. I was almost thirty-two when I met your mother. And, in your case, you can be sure that your parents, unlike mine, will not interfere when you want to marry.

I have one other thing to say to you. As far as your professional future is concerned, your mother being a producer and your father a director of films, you will have no trouble finding work. I want to ask you to think about this and to organize your life and studies effectively to achieve success later on.

Others see you as an adult, but I still see you as a baby wrestling with dreams. Life is difficult and complicated and one must learn to dominate it before it gets the upper hand.

Your old father wants to teach you a proverb that has much wisdom: *he is most intelligent who protects himself*. You're not going to tell me that's outmoded too! In any case, learn how to reach your objective without destroying yourself.

They also say that *one has to know how to shout if*

one wants to shake up the world. That means that if you gain some success, the public will overlook your past, no matter how mediocre it is.

I am confident that you will regain your morale and begin a splendid life. Your father loves you very much and supports you. If you fall, there's always time to get up again. And if you're not strong enough to do it by yourself, all you have to do is to knock on my door: I'll always reach out my hand to you.

My heart is linked to yours. When you walk, I take a step; when you weep, I weep too.

There, that's all I wanted to tell you. I ask you once more to forgive your parents. We are thinking of you and expecting your good news.

Your father,
who loves you more than anyone in the world.

This letter wiped away all my unhappiness. I felt filled with enormous power. I answered my father very quickly, thanking him and announcing that I had decided to leave China in order to acquire more experience. One day I would return to renew my struggle with increased energy, because it was to my country alone that I wanted to give the best of myself.

Papa sent me another letter. He regretted my decision; he would have liked us to make films together. He added, however, that he would not oppose my plans, "When you lose your way," he wrote, "I'll be there with my light to guide you and when you succeed, I will offer you flowers."

I no longer felt miserable. I was rich in my family's love.

Chapter 28

YANN

One Saturday afternoon, a Frenchwoman I knew invited me to an evening get-together that sounded pleasant. At first the atmosphere there seemed rather disappointing. There were only a few Chinese; most of the people were French, English and American businessmen and the conversation was in English, which I didn't know well, so I made no effort to join in. My French acquaintance was friendly but she turned out to be something of a bore. She kept asking me tedious, meaningless questions — "Why do the Chinese eat so much rice?" "Do the Chinese ever joke around?" — and finally exasperated me to the point that I decided to leave. But then she introduced me to one of her friends, a French photographer. Finally here was someone who was not a businessman. He was not very tall, but his golden hair fascinated me.

He said his name was Yann which, he explained to me in perfect Chinese, meant "Thunder Devil" in our language. I burst out laughing, thinking how some Chinese must have made fun of him, sticking him with such a ridiculous name; he himself seemed very proud of it. When I told him that my name meant "Sourpuss," it was his turn to laugh.

From our very first words, I felt strongly drawn to him. Wanting to prolong the conversation, I asked him questions I knew the answers to, thanks to what my hostess had told me. I feigned surprise and admiration every time he opened his mouth. He was so interesting that we talked for two hours. When he had to leave, I had a twinge of sadness, feeling as if I had known him for a long time.

I had invited him to a preview of a movie by a friend of my father's. He accepted enthusiastically, while I returned home pleased with myself and sure that I would have beautiful dreams.

I got all dressed up in my best clothes. Yann arrived half an hour late. I was annoyed, but I couldn't stay angry with him — he was too charming. I was surprised that he knew my father's friend, the director of the film we were going to see. I was afraid that the director would tell my parents that I was going out with a foreigner, so I lied and told him that I knew Yann because he had given a talk at the university.

Either the film didn't interest him at all, or else he was very tired. In any case, he slept through it and then, to add to the rudeness, took my hand! I pulled it back quickly, begging him to behave properly . . . . He invited me to dinner afterwards and had the nerve to give me his opinion of the movie he had slept through. He said that he was able to watch films while he was asleep.

In spite of all this, and even though he told me that he had a girlfriend in Paris, we became good friends. His straight-forwardness had impressed me and made me somewhat starry-eyed. He would kiss me on the cheek, but never tried to go any further.

When he came back after two weeks in the provinces, Yann invited me to dinner and a movie; we went to see a video of *Casablanca*, his favorite film. He translated the dialogue and explained the significance of the images to me. I was in seventh heaven and I allowed myself to think that he might love me. I put my head on his shoulder and waited . . . but he said suddenly that he was going to take me home. I was fed up. No longer shy, I flatly announced that this evening I was going to stay with him. I didn't care whether I embarrased him.

It was the most marvelous night I had ever experienced. I loved his kisses, his caresses and, even more, his body and his scent.

I stayed for the weekend, washed his clothes, straightened his apartment and cooked him spectacular Chinese meals. I surprised myself; I had never done that for any boyfriend before. Later, I stopped worrying about the time I was spending or the risks I was running and rushed to be with him every time he called. Soon he knew all about me and about how I wanted to travel abroad. He listened sympathetically and I could tell that he understood me. Little by little, my joy in living returned. His tenderness warmed my heart, his sense of humor kept my black thoughts away and his wide interests enriched my mind.

I knew that someday he planned to rejoin his girlfriend in Paris; I had to accept the fact that I was little more than an interlude in his life. Still, everytime I said, "I like you," I heard a voice inside me saying "I love you" instead.

I had to leave Beijing to make a television film for the university. I had managed to get the professors to let me have Chang Ling and Kuo Kuo as part of my crew. We filmed at the seaside; it was the first time I had seen the sea and I loved it. If the water had not been so icy, I would have dived into it instantly.

The filming was a complete fiasco. Not only had the professors chosen an inept screenplay, but the weather was so cold people could hardly work. On top of that, we squabbled every day over the budget and Kuo Kuo deliberately refused to follow my instructions. One day I lost my temper and slapped him twice. He slapped me back, hard. If the camera had not fallen down in the confusion that followed, the whole thing would have ended up in a free-for-all. I became extremely conscious that we had a real problem with sexism: even though we were all young, no male would follow the directions of a female movie director.

When we got back to Beijing, I took the crew to dinner at a Mongolian restaurant. Afterward, they departed two-by-two, leaving me alone. Even Kuo Kuo, no doubt tired of running after me, had found a girlfriend.

I wandered alone through the grey streets of the capital, and finally decided to call Yann. Thank God he was at home and, being a little bit drunk, I almost died of happiness. We met at a bridge at the edge of the Forbidden City and went for a walk. He told me that he and his girlfriend had broken up. I was delighted, but he was very depressed; he said they had been together for seven years. I asked him whether he had left her for someone else. He said no, it was her decision.

What a boor! He could have told me that I was the cause! Inside my head I called him every sort of name for his unromantic attitude, but I felt sorry for him for having been dumped and tried to amuse him with all sorts of stories that I considered funny.

Without the specter of his Parisian girlfriend, our relationship became more relaxed and we behaved like a real couple.

Yann introduced me to his friends and invited me to official showings of his photographs. But he didn't declare his feelings. I wondered whether he considered me unattractive, or perhaps stupid. I decided to do everything I could to get him for myself.

I made a point to look attractive when I was going to see him and to take a special interest in his photographs. I even bought him flowers and gave him massages. When he walked around Beijing taking pictures, I was behind him, carrying his extremely heavy equipment. I felt euphoric, even though my feet and back were aching. So that he wouldn't feel that I was overdoing it, I never told him that I loved him. Slowly but surely, I thought I detected a certain look in his eyes; I thought I was making headway. I was ecstatic when he asked me to go with him to Shanghai where he was going with a group of French painters.

I invented a story to appease the administration, and two weeks later, with beating heart, finally landed in that city that opens out to the sea. Everything went swimmingly, except that, being Chinese, I was not permitted to stay in hotels meant for foreigners. I had to pass myself off as an interpreter for Yann's group. At night, as soon as the bellhops went to bed, I would creep into Yann's room and leave the next morning before the vigilant bellhops started their shift.

I had never seen foreigners working as a group. Their freedom and lack of sexism made me envious. I remembered my own experience working with the male students at the university. One evening I became so depressed about the frustration I had to live with that, alone in my room, I burst into tears. Yann walked in and asked me what was wrong. I told him that I wanted so much to be like the Westerners; at the same time, I was afraid I really was the bad girl people said I was. Yann told me not to cry. He said that China was very conservative, and that in other countries people wouldn't judge me like that.

This didn't make me feel better; in fact, it made me feel worse. Maybe he was right, but what he said was too far removed from my experience. Knowing about life in foreign countries couldn't change my existence in China. Few Chinese could understand me, so how could a foreigner?

"Niu-Niu," he said, "ever since you told me your story, I've given it a lot of thought and I've decided to help you come to France."

This made me furious. "How dare you make fun of me! First of all, you don't love me and, second of all, you don't want to get married. So what's the point!"

"It's true that I don't want to marry, but that doesn't mean that I don't love you . . ."

At last, he convinced me that he was sincere. When our trip was over, I returned to the university, feeling that I could trust him.

I found a letter from my parents waiting for me on my dormitory bed. Somehow I expected good news. I hurriedly opened it. I couldn't believe what I read — my grandmother had died of a heart attack while I was in Shanghai. I didn't want to believe it. Grandma couldn't have left me. She had promised to wait to see my first film. I couldn't conceive of living without her. She had been my mother and I was a long way from giving back to her all that she had given me. I thought I must be responsible for her death, because of my foolishness, my depravity, because I wasn't there. No doubt she lay dying of unhappiness while I was selfishly enjoying myself in Shanghai. I would rather have died at once than know that I had killed her. I decided I would not go anywhere, nor would I ever see Yann again.

I wrote a letter to my parents confessing where I had been during these two regrettable weeks, that I had been in the company of a foreigner I was in love with. I added that I would stop seeing Yann to expiate the wrong I had done to Grandma. This nightmare lasted a whole month until my parents arrived in Beijing.

They picked me up in a taxi and brought me to their hotel room. They told me I shouldn't feel responsible for Grandmother's death; she had died because she was old. They knew that I loved her and they commented on how thin and pale I looked. Then they told me the real reason they had come to Beijing. They wanted to find out what Yann was like, to assure themselves that he was sincere and not just another foreigner taking advantage of a Chinese girl. My father was particularly happy that Yann was a photographer rather than an unimaginative businessman; a husband like that could help my career.

When I told him that Yann didn't want to get married, he said, "You're mad! How could you live together without being married?" After a considerable argument, during which I explained to them that the lifestyle of the West was gradually influencing the way young people lived in China, they finally agreed to meet Yann. "Now it's high time that I get a good look at this Frenchman!" my mother said. "If he's one of those you can't count on, even if you've slept together I would not give you to him."

We all went to dinner at Maxim's, an exact reproduction of the famous Parisian reataurant. Strangely enough, my parents didn't ask Yann a single question about our relationship. The conversation revolved almost entirely around film and photography. My father was eager for information about what was going on in the West. And Mama, despite the horror inspired by her bloody steak, confessed to me that she liked Yann very much. "If you love each other, this time your parents won't get in your way."

A week later I accompanied my parents to the station; they were loaded down with gifts from Yann. I thanked Heaven that they were so understanding.

Yann began the process of getting a passport for me. I had to give the police a letter from the university. When I went to the authorities to ask for it, it was obvious that I was in for new trouble. By simply making such a request I seemed to make them furious. They knew that I had lied in order to go to Shanghai, and they decided to use that to expel me from the university. I could attend class and stay in a dormitory, but only on condition that I pay for it and that I break off all contacts with foreigners. The consequences of this were clear: if I was not able to leave China, it would be impossible for me to find work or to enroll in another university. I no longer had a choice — I felt I had to go.

Ironically, my expulsion made my efforts to obtain a passport easier. Since all my documents had now been sent back to my native city where no one knew what I had done and said in Beijing, I did not have long to wait for the papers necessary for leaving the country. I felt halfway to freedom: all I needed now was a visa. My future was entirely in Yann's hands. The law required that he act as my financial guarantor.

He had to return to France; I spent a sleepless night before his flight. I couldn't help thinking that he wasn't coming back and that I would become another Madame Butterfly. As I was packing his bags, I gritted my teeth and held back my tears to seem strong. Yann appeared calm. He told me that he would phone me and that I could call him collect. At the airport the sound of his departing steps stabbed me like so many daggers. I returned to my dormitory, where I was now a paying guest, and prayed to God that Yann would come back for me.

 Chapter 29

RETURN OF THE THUNDER DEVIL

A month went by during which I went to the French Consulate every week to check on my visa. There wasn't any progress and so I stayed on at the university, attending classes and paying tuition for them.

The news of my expulsion had quickly spread throughout the campus; those who despised me no longer tried to hide it, while those who liked me were happy for me. I went to ask for a letter certifying that I had completed three years of study and to reclaim copies of the films I had made, but ran up against the departmental chairman's categorical refusal, on the pretext that I had been expelled. All at once it was as though my three years of study had never taken place. There was nothing I could do about this, so I tried to accept it.

I went cold with fright when Kuo Kuo told me that he had heard on good authority that the departmental chairman was going to send a report about me to the police, denouncing my behavior and my plans to leave the country.

He also said that Kao Lan and her friends were shouting from the housetops that I had bought my passport. All this was no joke. Even though Kuo Kuo reassured me that he had a friend with the police who would warn me in time, I was constantly on edge. When my visa still did not arrive, I began to have doubts about Yann. The poor man, who spent a fortune on long distance calls, had no inkling that only his presence could have reassured me.

My foreign friends seemed to lose all their civility and politeness with me. Their dinner and dance invitations were fraught with ulterior motives: they really wanted me to end up in their arms by the end of the evening. In this sex-obsessed environment I felt like a sheep surrounded by wolves. While foreigners and Chinese alike continued with their lives and their affairs, I was excluded from both. I felt I might as well throw out my books and pens; things that had brought happiness into my life. For no good reason, I turned down the starring role in a film directed by one of my father's friends. I was wasting my days.

Finally, to escape this deadly boredom, I allowed these oversexed foreign demons to take me out to dine and dance, even though I continued to deny them the diversion which they so eagerly looked forward to at the end of the evening.

I ran across Yann's friend Olivier, who had just returned from France, and I asked him whether he had any news about Yann. After an embarassed pause, he suggested that we go to his place to talk about it. There he told me that Yann was living with another girl, that he no longer loved me; in fact, he had forgotten all about me.

This justified all my doubts and anguish. I thought I would die from the shock. I was in agony. Fortunately Olivier chose this moment to go to the bathroom, and I gulped down two large whiskeys while holding my nose. The effect was immediate. My head was on fire, and I collapsed on the couch.

Through a dizzy blur, I saw Olivier staring at me strangely. I hated him for bringing me such deadly news but without understanding why I did it, I told him that I loved him . . . . He carried me to his bedroom. If Yann no longer loved me, I had no need to worry about anything.

From that night on, I went crazy, leading a chaotic life without love, without hope and without decency. I smoked and drank, went dancing every night, and passed from one lover to the next. When I woke up each morning, I hated myself, but after the first drink, I would begin all over again. I often left the phone off the hook. When Yann tried to reach me, I hung up on him.

At the university, Chang Ling and Kuo Kuo told me that because of my illicit relationships with foreigners, the police had come to question the professors about me and that I was going to be arrested. That same evening, I bought a train ticket to return to my parents. My luggage was going to be shipped to me soon afterwards by my friends.

I stayed alone at the house for two weeks, while my parents were working and my younger sister was staying with my uncle. I was at loose ends, spending my time sleeping or watching television. I was so bored and depressed that I decided to go back to Beijing, despite the danger that I ran there. I didn't care if the police caught me. The end was near for me, so why not have a good time before prison? Behind bars there would be no cigarettes, drinks, night-clubs . . . .

Yann called me at a friend's apartment where I was staying and I told him I wanted nothing more to do with him. I was distraught. He swore he had never lied to me and loved me despite my stupid behavior. Olivier was lying, he said. He told me to grow up and stop acting like an idiot. But I hung up on him. An hour later, thirsty for revenge, I went to Olivier's office and slapped him twice. Then, using the key that he had given me, I went to his apartment, and turned the whole place upside down.

The following day Yann called again. He had decided to come back to Beijing at once. When he arrived, we talked things over for three exhausting days; it became obvious that Olivier had deliberately misled me. Yann forgave me for my lack of trust and we reconciled at last.

Chapter 30
PARIS

To mark our departure, Yann invited my mother to Beijing to say goodbye to us. Unfortunately, my father's work kept him from coming. Yann had also invited my best friends, Kuo Kuo, Chang Ling, Nancy and a few others. He was perfectly familiar with Chinese customs, offering each one gifts as he thanked them for the help they had given me and insisting that they accept.

On the evening of the day before we were to leave, I went back to the university that I had already left long ago. Chang Ling, Kuo Kuo and I wandered through the classroom building, across the playing field and under the trees. As I strolled, it was as though I were seeing a film of the years that I had spent within those walls. I had learned more there in three years than in all the years of my life before. Dreams and nightmares were interwoven like the warp and woof of a fabric.

On the verge of leaving that place where I had lived such intense moments, I felt less hatred towards it, towards its professors and towards the students who had inflicted so much suffering on me. If it had not been for their hostile treatment, I would never have met Yann: misery has its silver lining.

After every banquet the guests go their separate ways: today it was I who was going away, tomorrow it might be Kuo Kuo's or Chang Ling's turn to leave. For the last time we were together dreaming of our future, hoping that one day we could meet again and be as cheerful as we were now.

It was under the stars of this calm evening with a night breeze gently blowing that I had to say goodbye to Chang Ling and Kuo Kuo. I had already said goodbye to Hsiao Ch'uan, Kao Lan and all the professors that I had known. Each step that took me toward the gate immersed me more deeply in my memories.

The next day, in the car on the road to the airport, my mother never stopped moaning about my going so far away and about how she and my father were not there to take care of me when I was small. I tried to comfort her by promising to be reasonable and to act like an adult.

The moment of separation arrived. Tears running down her face, Mama followed me with her eyes as she waved her handkerchief. I had a heavy heart.

After stopovers in Canton and Hong Kong, one week later, on the morning of November 17, 1986, I boarded the plane for Paris. When it had finally cleared the runway, I felt completely free and unburdened. I cried tears of joy, but at the same time I was wistful. I knew that I would come back some day. I would never forget my family, my friends, and my country. I would never forget that I was Chinese.

November 18, 1986, 10 a.m.: I arrive in Paris.

We leave the airport in Yann's wonderful car. I have the impression that we have hardly left the superhighway, when I find myself, as in a dream, on the top of the Eiffel Tower, with Paris at my feet. It is raining. I want to laugh, but find myself weeping with joy.

"Is this how France always looks?"

"It's even better than that, you'll see . . . . You're free, Niu-Niu."

Freedom — what a lovely word!